NOTES ON THE HEBREW TEXT
OF 2 SAMUEL XVI–XIX

NOTES ON THE HEBREW TEXT OF 2 SAMUEL XVI—XIX

BY

NORMAN H. SNAITH, M.A. (OXON)

Tutor in Old Testament Languages and Literature
in Wesley College, Headingley

An Abingdon importation

ABINGDON PRESS
New York   Nashville

EXCLUSIVE DISTRIBUTOR FOR U.S.A.

Price $1

Made and Printed in Great Britain by
The Camelot Press Ltd., London and Southampton

PREFACE

THESE notes are designed particularly for beginners who may be studying these chapters as their first Hebrew Text. Especially are they designed for students whose circumstances compel them to study by themselves, without being in touch with anyone who can guide them in regular tuition. References are given, wherever necessary, to the germane pages in Davidson's *Introductory Hebrew Grammar*, 20th and later editions (reference, DG), and to Wood and Lanchester's *A Hebrew Grammar* (WL), these being the grammars most in use by elementary students. Further references are given to Davidson's *Hebrew Syntax* (DS), Gesenius-Kautzsch (GK, by paragraphs), Driver's *Hebrew Tenses* (DT), and also to the two Commentaries on the Hebrew Text of Samuel, Driver's *Notes on the Hebrew Text of the Books of Samuel*, 2nd Ed. (Dr, a book which every student is recommended to study) and the I.C.C. Commentary by H. P. Smith (ICC). BDB means the *Oxford Lexicon*, by Brown, Driver and Briggs. HDB is Hastings' *Dictionary of the Bible*. EB is *Encyclopaedia Biblica*. Every care has been taken to ensure complete accuracy.

N. H. S.

February, 1945.

CHAPTER XVI

Verse 1. ‏ודוד עבר‏. The *vav*-consecutive construction
is here broken, because the narrative turns away from
Absalom to David. We get therefore the subject put
first, and the verb (now in the perfect) coming second,
DG 84–6, WL 88–91. Translate 'Now David had
crossed (passed) over . . .'

‏מעט‏, 'a little while'. It is an adverb of time, not
of place. If it is to be regarded as an adverb of place
here (as Dr 318, and presumably EVV), then it is
unique.

‏מהראש‏, 'from the summit (ridge, lit. "head")'.
The prep. ‏מן‏ (from) with short vowel expanding into
tsere before a guttural which cannot be doubled,
DG 52, WL 20, § 3 (b).

‏בשת‏, *bosheth* (shame) is a pious substitution by the
scribes, even as early as LXX, to avoid the use of
the name Baal, Dr 253 *f*, HDB i. 209, ERE ii. 283 *ff*.
The name was originally Merib-baal, as in 1 Chronicles
viii. 34, ix. 40.

‏לקראתו‏, prep. *lamedh* (purpose) plus inf. cstr. qal
of ‏קרא‏ (meet) plus 3 m. s. suff. There is confusion
between the two roots ‏קרא‏ I (call, read aloud)
and ‏קרא‏ II = (properly) ‏קרה‏ (meet), DG 125. For
the cstr. infs., ‏לִקְרַאת‏ means 'to meet', WL 182,
and ‏לִקְרֹא‏ or ‏לִקְרֹאות‏ 'to call'.

‏צמד‏ (pair, couple), but Klostermann suggested
‏וְעִמּוֹ‏, 'and with him (i.e. accompanying him)', which
is more suitable.

‏חבשים‏, m. p. pass. ptc. qal of ‏חבש‏ (bind, and so
'laden').

7

הנה יושב. The use of הנה with the participle without the subject expressed is most unusual, and can be excused (if at all) only on the ground that the subject referred to immediately precedes; cf. Dr 134, GK 116 *q*.

בירושלם, prep. *beth* plus noun. The short *chireq* followed by *yod*-with-*sheva* has become a long *-i* written full, DG 51, WL 43.

כי, like דֿו, can be either a conjunction introducing indirect speech and even direct speech or a causal particle, as here.

היום (to-day), lit. 'the day' as in North-Country dialect.

ישיבו 3 m. p. impf. hiph. of שׁוּב (return), normal *ayin-vav* form. The subject is the collective sing., 'the house of Israel'.

ממלכות. This s. cstr. occurs nine times, of which five are in Joshua xiii and one in 1 Samuel xv. 28. Some would restore the form מַמְלֶכֶת generally, but it is better to regard the form as a conflation of מַלְכוּת and מַמְלֶכֶת (cstr. s. of מַמְלָכָה, DG 102, WL 96), both of which are sound forms.

אבי, 1 s. suff. of אב (father), one of a number of very common irregular nouns which must be known, DG 153, WL 185*f*.

Verse 4. השתחויתי, 1 s. pf. *hithpa'lel* of שׁחה (bow down). This curious verb is found 170 times, and is due to the reduplication of the last radical, the original *vav* being retained and the *he* being added, DG 145, WL 145, GK 75 *kk*. Usually the *vav* has become a *he* in Hebrew, and we have a normal *lamedh-he* verb. In addition, the *shin* and the *tau* have changed places, DG 93, WL 72. Notice especially the curious apocopated form. Notice also the *tsere*,

which occurs properly in all passive perfects of
lamedh-he verbs, and in all 1 s. perfects, except the
qal, whether active or passive, DG 229 (note),
WL 143. Translate 'I bow down . . .', being perfect
of action just completed, DS 60 (§ 40*b*).

אמצא, 1 s. impf. (Cohortative) qal of מצא (find),
normal *lamedh-aleph* verb. The true cohortative ending in a toneless *-ah* is not found in *lamedh-aleph*
verbs, presumably because of the difficulty of pro-
nouncing it. Translate 'let me find favour . . .'

המלך. The article denotes the vocative, as in
EVV, GK 126 *f*.

Verse 5. ובא. This form occurs at the beginning
of a verse 17 times, but this is the only case where
it is 3 m. s. pf. qal of בוא (come) with weak-*vav*.
Everywhere else it is with strong-*vav*, and is therefore
a good Hebrew construction. Either read וַיָּבֹא
(3 m. s. imf. qal with strong-*vav*) or assume that the
text is an unusual variant for the order והמלך דוד בא.
It is quite possible that both the author and the
Masoretes could not decide which of these two was
better in this particular case.

עד, 'as far as' or 'up to'. The distinction between
אֶל (to) and עַד (up to, as far as) can be slight, but
there are cases, such as this, where it is worth while.

בחורים. The *cheth* is virtually doubled, hence
the firm *pathach*. Otherwise the first vowel would be
vocal *sheva*.

ממשפחת, prep. מִן plus cstr. s. of מִשְׁפָּחָה (clan).

וּשְׁמוֹ שִׁמְעִי בֶן־גֵּרָא, 'and his name (was) Shimei-ben-
Gera', a little circumstantial clause, characteristic of
the best Hebrew style.

יֹצֵא יָצוֹא וּמְקַלֵּל, 'keeping on coming out and
cursing'. The three words are act. ptc. qal and inf.

abs. qal of יָצָא (go out, come out) and *vav* plus piel ptc. of קלל (curse). The more usual construction would be יֹצֵא יָצוֹא וְקַלֵּל with two inf. absolutes; e.g. 1 Samuel vi. 12; 2 Samuel iii. 16; see DS 119, WL 101, GK 113*s*, Dr 56.

Verse 6. וַיְסַקֵּל, strong-*vav* plus 3 m. s. impf. piel of סקל (stone); the *dagesh* fails in *yod*-with-*sheva*, as usual, DG 33, WL 20 and 90 (note 3).

בָּאֲבָנִים, with the article, as normally thus in Hebrew. They were not any indefinite stones, but the particular definite stones which he did throw, GK 126*q–t*, DS 26.

מִימִינוֹ וּמִשְּׂמֹאלוֹ, prep. מִן plus יָמִין (right) plus 3 m. s. suff., followed by *vav* (and) plus prep. מִן plus שְׂמֹאל (left) plus 3 m. s. suff.; in English idiom, 'right and left', unless he threw with both hands (ICC 348). In the first word the *nun* of the prep. מִן has assimilated to the following *yod*, then the *dagesh* has failed in *yod*-with-*sheva*, and finally the *yod*-with-*sheva* plus the short *chireq* has become a long *chireq*, DG 52 (top), WL 43.

Verse 7. בְּקַלְלוֹ, prep. *beth* plus inf. cstr. piel plus 3 m. s. suff., lit. 'in his cursing', but see EVV. The piel-*dagesh* fails in *lamedh*-with-*sheva*, DG 32*f*, WL 20.

צֵא, 2 m. s. imperat. qal of יצא (go out, come out), one of six *pe-yod* verbs like יֵשֵׁב. They are: 'When Adam *knew* ידע that Eve *had borne* ילד a son, he *went out* יצא of the house, *went down* ירד the steps, *went for a walk* הלך in' the Garden (i.e. of Eden), and *sat* ישב under the apple-tree.'

דָּמִים. The plural of דָּם is used of shed blood. The article in this and the following construct phrase is for the vocative, GK 126*e*, DS 27.

בְלִיַעל. A compound of בְּלִי (noun 'wearing-out' used as negative) and יַעַל (worth, use, profit), and meaning 'worthlessness'; the whole phrase is a term of virulent abuse.

Verse 8. הֵשִׁיב, 3 m. s. pf. hiph. of שׁוּב (return), and so transitive, the qal being intransitive. A normal *ayin-vav* form.

עָלֶיךָ, prep. עַל plus 2 m. s. suff., looking like a plural form, DG 70, WL 64 *f.*

אֲשֶׁר. Remember always that this is a relative and not a pronoun. In cases where it can be translated 'who', the subject must be understood as included in the verb, and not in the relative.

תחתו. The Qere has the normal form תַּחְתָּיו. The grammars say that this is a plural form, and similarly for suffixes of אַחֲרֵי (after); but this is not the case. They are actually duals, the reference being to a man's two feet and two buttocks. The Kethib here is probably תַּחְתּוֹ, a singular form.

וַיִּתֵּן, strong-*vav* plus 3 m. s. impf. qal of נתן (give). This verb is one of the very few really irregular verbs in Hebrew, and must be learned separately, DG 213, WL 255.

בנך. Pausal form with tone retracted, and therefore no need to change the vocal *sheva* under the *beth* into *chireq* before another vocal *sheva* (3rd declension). The normal form of בֵּן with 2 m. s. suff. is בִּנְךָ, DG 153, WL 186.

הנך, *vav* plus הִנֵּה plus 2 m. s. suff. The suffix is always added, except for the 3 m. s., which is properly הִנֵּה הוּא, though suffix forms are found, DG 142 (note), WL 110 *f*, GK 100 *s*, 147 *b*.

ברעתך, *beth* plus 2 m. s. suff. of sing. of רָעָה, but

with tone retracted in pause under *zaqeph qaton* (little *zaqeph*). Notice the firm *qamets* under *resh*, which is compensation, because the root is double-*ayin*, and the actual *ayin* cannot be doubled.

אַתָּה, pausal form with tone retracted and *pathach* lengthened into *qamets*, WL 117; cf. DG 40. The emphasis is thus on both 'a man of blood', because it comes first, and on the pronoun, because of the pause. In English we obtain the required emphasis by saying the whole phrase deliberately.

Verse 9. למה (why?), composed of prep. *lamedh* plus interrog. מה (what?). Generally the form is לָמָּה before gutturals *aleph* (including the Sacred Name), *he* and *ayin*, but otherwise לָמָּה , and always before *cheth*. For the seven exceptions, with four anomalous cases, GK 102*l*, BDB 554*a*.

יְקַלֵּל, 3 m. s. impf. piel of קלל (be light), but piel and pual of this root mean 'curse', since it must be done thoroughly if it is done at all. Translate 'why should . . . curse . . .'

המת, article plus act. ptc. qal of מוּת (die).

אעברה, 1 s. cohortative qal of עבר (cross over), followed by particle of entreaty.

ואסירה, weak-*vav* plus 1 sing. cohortative hiphil of סוּר. The qal is intransitive and means 'turn aside', whilst the hiphil is transitive as here, and is the common word for 'remove, take away'. The weak *vav* plus cohortative often equals the Greek ἵνα, DS 199.

Verse 10. מה-לי ולכם, 'What have I to do with ye?' lit. 'what to me and to ye'. Cf. John ii. 4, τί ἐμοὶ καὶ σοί.

14

כִּי . . . וכי. The Kethib is כִּי . . . וְכִי, but the Qere is כֹּה . . . כִּי. The Kethib is to be translated, 'If he curseth, and if the Lord hath said to him, "Curse David," then who shall say . . . ?' The Qere (which makes better sense) is: 'So let him curse, for the Lord hath said . . . and who shall say . . . ?' For conditional sentences, see WL 205, DS 175–9, especially § 130 (a) and (with כי instead of אם in the protasis), 178 Rem. 1; also GK 159, especially 159*r* and *bb*. The Greek Versions (LXX and Lucian) both have καὶ ἄφετε αὐτὸν, whence Klostermann, Smend, Budde, and ICC prefer הַנִּחוּ לוֹ (leave him), and then they follow (partly) LXX, καὶ οὕτως (Qere) καταράσθω ὅτι (Qere), reading וִיקַלֵּל כִּי (and let him curse, because . . .).

יאמר, 3 m. s. impf. qal of אמר (say), without tone retracted (note the *pathach*).

עשׂיתה, 2 m. s. pf. qal of עשׂה (do), with final vowel written full with *he*. This particular form occurs five times.

Verse 11. בני, 1 s. suff. to sing. of בֵּן (son), DG 153, WL 186. It is a third declension form, of which the first syllable cannot be touched because it is not there.

ממעי, prep. מִן plus 1 s. suff. to the plural מֵעִים (inward parts, intestines, bowels). The sing. (presumably מֵעָה) is not found, nor is the plural absolute, but only the plural in construct and with suffixes.

מבקשׁ, m. s. ptc. piel בקשׁ (seek); only the intensive forms are found, since every search is intensive in its degree.

נפשׁי, 1 s. suff. to sing. נֶפֶשׁ (here 'life'). This word should never be translated 'soul' in the O.T., except in our sense of individual. The normal sense of 'soul' is Greek, and not Hebrew.

אַף, at its strongest, is a strong asserative, as here, especially when it is strengthened by כִּי into 'how much more'. At its weakest, אַף means 'yes, and', as against אַךְ, 'yes, but'.

בֶּן־הַיְמִינִי, 'the Benjamite', i.e. this particular Benjamite, so the insertion by EVV of 'this' is sound for the English idiom. The phrase is regarded as a true construct, and therefore the article is added to the second member, WL 61. The *dagesh* has failed in *yod-with-sheva*, and the final syllable is normal for Gentilic names, DG 56.

הַנִּחוּ, 2 m. pl. imperat. hiph. of נוּחַ (rest). There are two hiphil forms of this verb: (A), the normal *ayin-vav* form הֵנִיחַ (impf. יָנִיחַ) with the true hiphil meaning 'to cause to rest' (of persons); (B) the form הִנִּיחַ (impf. יַנִּיחַ), meaning 'to deposit, let lie' (of things) and 'leave, let alone' (of persons).

וִיקַלֵּל, weak-*vav* plus 3 m. s. impf. (jussive) piel of קלל (curse). The *dagesh* has failed in *yod*-with-*sheva* and the short-*chireq* with *sheva* has lengthened into long-*chireq*, 'and let him curse'.

Verse 12. יִרְאֶה, 3 m. s. impf. qal of ראה (see), '(perhaps the Lord) may look upon (see following *beth*)'.

בעוני. The Kethib is בַּעֲוֹנִי, 'upon my iniquity', which is said (Dr 319, ICC 349) to mean 'upon the iniquity done to me', though it is recognized that this meaning is contrary to analogy. It is better to translate 'my punishment', e.g. Genesis iv. 13, or 'my suffering' (guilty or not guilty), the idea being that God will regard this additional punishment as

16

'satisfaction' and that it will be 'accepted' (cf. Isaiah xl. 2). LXX, Syr., and V presuppose בְּעָנְיִי (on my affliction), which many prefer. The Qere is בְּעֵינִי (upon my eye), which the Rabbis interpreted to mean 'upon my tears'; cf. AV margin.

וְהֵשִׁיב, strong-*vav* plus 3 m. s. pf. hiph. of שׁוּב (return), the hiphil being the transitive form as against the intransitive qal.

טוֹבָה, 'benefit, good things'. This fem. form is much more common in this sense than the masc.

קִלְלָתוֹ, 3 m. s. suff. to sing. קְלָלָה (his curse). This is the better reading, though some printed texts have Kethib, קִלְלָתִי (his cursing *me*) and the other as Qere.

Verse 13. וַיֵּלֶךְ, strong-*vav* plus 3 m. s. impf. qal of הלך (go), with tone retracted and last vowel shortened as often with strong-*vav* impf. One of six *pe-yod* verbs like וַיֵּשֶׁב.

וַאֲנָשָׁיו, *vav* plus 3 m. s. suff. to אֲנָשִׁים, plural of אִישׁ (man), DG 153, WL 185.

בדרך, prep. *beth* plus article plus דֶּרֶךְ in pause with *athnach*. The word is the most general word for 'road' (Lat., *iter*), though it particularly refers to a well-known route (cf. *iter*), especially a caravan route, e.g. 'the way of the Philistines', Exodus xiii. 17. מְסִלָּה is a raised highway (Lat., *via*), a Class-A road, as against אֹרַח, which is 'path' (Lat., *semita*), perhaps at its best a Class C road. נְתִיבָה is also a raised road, but is chiefly poetical, and with a general significance, though perhaps a Class B road.

בצלע, prep. *beth* plus a cstr. s. form of צֵלָע (rib, and so 'side' generally, the root meaning 'curved').

The abs. sing is as if 1st declension, but other sing. forms are segholate forms, the construct being צֶלַע (as here uniquely) or צֵלַע. The plural is once with -*im* and masculine (and so apparently Exodus xxvi. 34), but otherwise in -*oth* and feminine. Some of these 'plural' forms are probably duals.

לעמתו. The word עֻמָּה is a noun signifying juxta-position, and in every case, except the late Ecclesiastes v. 15, is found with the prep. *lamedh* and with suffix (once sing. cstr., Ecclesiastes, v. 15 and once pl. cstr., Ezekiel xlv. 7). The meaning is not 'over against' as in EVV, but 'side by side with . . .', 'parallel to . . .'

ויקלל ויסקל, strong-*vav* plus 3 m. s. impf. piel (twice), one of קלל (curse) and the other of סקל (cast stones). The normal construction would have been הלֹךְ . . . הָלוֹךְ, followed by two inf. absolutes, וְקַלֵּל וְסַקֵּל, and so most scholars read; cf. another variation from the normal construction in verse 5. Possibly it is better to omit הלוך, as Syriac does, and let the other tenses stand.

באבנים, again with *beth* and the article, as in verse 6.

לעמתו (second) is awkward, and is best omitted, though it is evident that LXX read some word here. LXX (cod. B), ἐκ πλαγίων αὐτοῦ, and Lucian and Syriac, ἐπ' ἀυτόν.

וְעִפֵּר. Presumably this is strong-*vav* plus 3 m. s. pf. piel of denominative עפר (to make dust) from noun עָפָר (dust), which is here used as a cognate accusative. Many would follow the previous alterations by reading inf. abs. piel here, וְעַפֵּר. Translate the text: 'and he kept on throwing dust'.

בעפר, here also the prep. *beth* plus the article, as before.

Verse 14. וַיָּבֹא, strong-*vav* plus 3 m. s. impf. qal of בּוֹא (come).

אתו, prep. אֵת (with) plus 3 m. s. suff. It is necessary carefully to distinguish between this word and (אֶת-) אֵת, which is the sign of the accusative, plus suffix. Similarly for both words with other suffixes, DG 75 and 142, WL 49. The prep. comes from an original אִנְתְּ, and therefore always has אֵת with suffixes, the *nun* having coalesced.

עיפים, m. p. of adjective עָיֵף (weary). A place-name is missing here, and some such reference is certainly required. Lucian inserts παρὰ τὸν ʼΙορδάνην (beyond Jordan), which may be an intelligent gloss. Klostermann suggested an original עַד־עָפְנִי (as far as Ophni), Joshua xviii. 24; ICC suggests עַבְרוֹת הַמִּדְבָּר (the fords of the wilderness; cf. xv. 28, xvii. 16), but, in view of Lucian's reading, we suggest עַבְרוֹת הַיַּרְדֵּן (the fords of the Jordan), which is an alternative name.

וינפש, strong-*vav* plus 3 m. s. impf. niph. of נפש, denominative verb from נֶפֶשׁ, meaning 'refresh' in Syriac. Translate 'and he refreshed himself there'. The verb occurs only here and Exodus xxiii. 13 (E), xxxi. 17 (P). The tone is retracted, and final *tsere* reduced to *seghol*.

Verse 15. The point of interest changes, and the *vav*-consecutive sequence breaks down.

העם (the people). The word is superfluous and creates difficulty. It is best omitted as an accidental repetition from the previous verse. It is not in LXX.

In this story כָּל־הָעָם (all the people) are with David, and כָּל־אִישׁ יִשְׂרָאֵל (every man of Israel) with Absalom (Dr 319).

Verse 16. וַיְהִי strong-*vav* plus 3 m. s. apoc. impf. qal of הִיָה (to be, but more accurately 'to become'). 'And it came to pass', whence NT καὶ ἐγένετο. For apocopated forms of *lamedh-he* verbs, see DG 147, WL 144. Pronounce *wăy-yᵉ-hî*. The *dagesh forte* of the strong-*vav* fails, as usual in *yod*-with-*sheva* (DG 147f, WL 20), but it is better always to pronounce as if it is there.

בָּא, 3 m. s. pf. qal, but here to be translated as a pluperfect, the action having taken place before that of the main verb.

רֵעֶה דָוִד, 'the friend of David', evidently some special title. The cstr. s. ending in *seghol* רֵעֶה is strange, since this form is the abs. s. It is nevertheless a sound reading always in this phrase, and is expressly mentioned by the Masorah. The normal cstr. s. of a masc. *lamedh-he* noun ends in *tsere*, GK 93*ll*, DG 148, WL 189.

יְחִי הַמֶּלֶךְ, 'Long live the king', lit. 'let the king live'. The phrase is repeated in the Hebrew, but not in LXX. יְחִי is 3 m. s. apoc. impf. (jussive) qal of חיה (live); see DG 147f, WL 145 (and note).

Verse 17. חַסְדְּךָ, 2 m. s. suff. plus sing. חֶסֶד. This word is usually translated 'loving-kindness, mercy', but it is essentially a covenant word, and here means 'loyalty'. See *Exp. Times*, July, 1941, p. 395.

אֵת. It is best to regard this as the sign of the 'accusative', רֵעֲךָ being in loose subordination to what precedes.

רֵעֲךָ, 2 m. s. suff. plus sing. of רֵעַ (friend), which

20

is a shortened and more usual form of רָעֶה (previous verse). This form varies between רֵעֲךָ and רֵעֶךָ, short for רְעֶיךָ (2 Samuel xii. 11), where the original *yod* (for *he*) is preserved. The first part of Absalom's remark to Hushai can be taken either as a question (so most), 'Is this your loyalty . . . ?' or as a caustic comment, 'So this is . . .'

Verse 18. לֹא, 'No'. There is a complete break after this word, indicated by *zaqeph-gadhol* (big *zaqeph*).

לֹא, (second) Kethib, but the Qere and the Versions have לוֹ (to him). The confusion is probably due to an attempt to avoid the suggestion that God could ever choose any other than the true Davidic king. Translate 'his will I be, and with him will I stay'. Compare Herod's speech to Octavian at Rhodes, Josephus, *Antiq.*, xv, 187–93.

אֵשֵׁב, 1 s. impf. qal of יָשַׁב (dwell, sit, stay). One of the six special *pe-yod* verbs.

Verse 19. וְהַשֵּׁנִית, *vav* plus article plus ordinal, 'and secondly', lit. 'and the second (thing) is . . .'

לְמִי, prep. *lamedh* plus interrog. 'who?' The verb עבד sometimes takes a direct, and sometimes an indirect object.

עֲבַדְתִּי. Perhaps this should be עָמַדְתִּי (stand); cf. Elijah in 1 Kings xviii. 15, etc., 'before whom I stand' (Ehrlich). לִפְנֵי is certainly curious with the verb עבד.

אָבִיךָ, 2 m. s. suff. plus sing. אָב (father), DG 153, WL 185.

אֶהְיֶה, 1 s. impf. qal of היה (to be). The first syllable is open.

Verse 20. הָבוּ, 2 m. p. imperat. qal of יהב (give). This verb is the ordinary Aramaic and Syriac equivalent of the Hebrew נתן, but is found in

21

Hebrew only in the imperat. qal. The *qamets* is anomalous, since the normal *pe-yod* form would be הַבוּ. This lengthening of the *chateph-pathach* is a feature of this curiously surviving imperative, GK 69*o*, BDB 396*b*. The following לכם is idiomatic, Deuteronomy i. 13; Joshua xviii. 4; Judges xx. 7 (GK 119*s*). It is doubtful whether ICC is right in saying that Absalom is addressing the whole circle of counsellors.

נעשׂה, 1 pl. impf. qal of עשׂה (do), *pe*-guttural and *lamedh-he* verb.

Verse 21. בוא, 2 m. s. imperat. qal בּוֹא (come, but here 'enter, go in').

פלנשי, cstr. pl. of פִּלֶגֶשׁ, sometimes written with *yod* in first syllable, since the *chireq* is unchangeable, and is long. It is probably a Greek word, introduced into Asia by Phoenician merchants. The word originally is connected with the name of the goddess Pallas, and meant 'virgin-priestess', but came to mean a captive or bought slave (παλλακή), as distinguished from a lawful wife, whence the form παλλακίς means a concubine, mistress, again as opposed to the lawful wife; cf. Lat. *pellex*.

הניח, 3 m. s. pf. hiph. (second form) of נוּח (rest). This is a true perfect '(whom) he has left . . .'. See verse 11.

לשׁמור, *lamedh* (purpose) plus inf. cstr. qal of שׁמר (keep, guard). The first syllable is closed, DG 77 (§ 2, ii), WL 100.

הבית, article plus בַּיִת (house), with *pathach* lengthened to *qamets* is pause with *athnach*, DG 153, WL 186.

ושׁמע, strong-*vav* plus 3 m. s. pf. qal, 'and (all Israel) will hear'.

נבאשׁת, 2 m. s. pf. niph. of בָּאַשׁ (to stink), '(that)

22

thou hast made thyself odious (with) . . .', but LXX
has κατήσχυνας τὸν πατέρα σου, whence many
would read הֲבִישֹׁתָ, 2 m. s. pf. hiph. of בּוֹשׁ (to be
ashamed), i.e. 'that thou hast put (thy father) to
shame . . .'

וְחָזְקוּ, strong-*vav* plus 3 p. pf. qal of חָזַק (to be
strong).

יְדֵי, cstr. dual of יָד (hand). Note that the dual
יָדַיִם is used of hands in pairs, but the plural יָדוֹת
of hands that are not pairs.

אִתָּךְ, prep. אֵת (with) plus 2 m. s. suff. pausal
form for the normal אִתְּךָ, DG 142, WL 49. The
m. pausal form is similar to the normal fem.

Verse 22. וַיֵּטוּ, strong-*vav* plus 3 m. p. impf. hiph.
of נטה (stretch out, incline), *pe-nun* and *lamedh-he*
verb. Here used of pitching a tent.

הָאֹהֶל, article plus אֹהֶל (tent), the bridal tent of
the Semites, חֻפָּה.

הַגַּב, article plus גַּב (roof). The plural is גַּבּוֹת,
since the word is a double assimilation of גַּנְבַּן,
a reduplicated form from גַּן (garden), i.e. a roof
garden, originally a covered garden. Similarly *pathach*
with doubled *gimel* for sing. suffixes.

לְעֵינֵי, prep. *lamedh* plus cstr. dual of עַיִן (eye), 'in
the sight of'.

Verse 23. וַעֲצַת, *vav* plus cstr. s. of עֵצָה (counsel),
from root יעץ.

בַּיָּמִים, prep. *beth* plus article plus pl. of יוֹם (day),
DG 153, WL 186.

הָהֵמָּה, article plus demonstrative adjective m. pl.
Note the *qamets* contrary to rule, DG 47, WL 36.

כאשר, 'as if, as when', the אֲשֶׁר turns the prep. into a conjunction.

יִשְׁאַל, 3 m. s. impf. qal of שָׁאַל (ask); understand either אִישׁ as the Qere), 'as if a man were to ask ...', or הַשֹּׁאֵל, 'as if the asker were to ask ...'. Usually this verb, though it can take a direct object, has prep. *lamedh* for person and prep. *beth* for instrument.

CHAPTER XVII

Verse 1. אבחרה, 1 s. cohort. qal of בחר (chose). In the best texts this word has the accent *munach*, and there is no *maqqeph*. After the particle of entreaty (נא), insert לִי, after LXX. This 'dative of advantage' is idiomatic with this verb, GK 119*s*. 'Let me, I pray, choose me ...'.

שְׁנִים עָשָׂר, 'twelve'. All the masculine cardinals from 12 to 19 are formed of the number 10 in the masc. abs. עָשָׂר preceded by the feminine absolute of the second digit, except for 12, where it is the masculine mixed form שְׁנֵים (the true masc. cstr. שְׁנֵי being found six times only). The corresponding feminine cardinals have the fem. form עֶשְׂרֵה for the first digit plus the masc. cstr. form for the second, except again for 12, when it is the fem. mixed form שְׁתֵּים (the true fem. cstr. שְׁתֵּי being found four times only, three of them in Ezekiel), GK 97*d*. Lucian reads 10,000 here, but that cannot be the original Hebrew reading, since the Hebrew for 10,000 is רְבָבָה, and not עָשָׂר אֶלֶף.

וָאֲקוּמָה, weak-*vav* plus 1 s. cohortative (with

24

toneless *he*, as always for *ayin-vav* and double-*ayin* verbs) qal of קוּם (rise up). This and the following weak-*vav*-plus-cohortative are both equal to the Greek ἵνα.

אַחֲרֵי, prep. 'after'. It is a dual form, and not plural.

הַלַּיְלָה, article plus לַיְלָה (night), with *pathach* lengthened to *qamets* in pause with *silluq* at the end of the verse. Idiomatic 'the night' (cf. North-Country idiom) for 'to-night'.

Verse 2. וְאָבוֹא, weak-*vav* plus 1 s. impf. (equal cohortative for *lamedh-alpeh* verb) of בּוֹא (come), 'that I may arise and pursue . . . (2) and come upon . . .'

. . . וְהוּא יָגֵעַ, lit. 'and he weary and weak of hands', and idiomatic circumstantial clause (GK 141*e*, DT 201, DS 185–9) in the best Hebrew style. In English, 'whilst he is weary . . .'

רְפֵה, cstr. s. masc. of adj. רָפֶה (weak, slack). Note that m. abs. s. is רָפֶה; m. cstr. s. is רְפֵה; f. abs. s. is רָפָה.

וְהַחֲרַדְתִּי, strong-*vav* plus 1 s. pf. hiph. of חרד (to be terrified). The writer has slipped at last into the *vav*-consecutive narrative tense. Note that the tone is thrown forward on to the last syllable, DG 86, WL 90 (note, but it is true of the 1 sing. also). Note that the effect of moving the tone further away from the guttural-with-*chateph* is to change the 'baby-*e*' to a 'baby-*a*', the normal 1 s. pf. hiph. being הֶחֱרַדְתִּי. Actually the change is made whether the tone is thrown forward or not, Dr 126.

וְנָס, strong-*vav* plus 3 m. s. pf. qal of נוּס (flee).

וְהִכֵּיתִי, strong-*vav* plus 1 s. pf. hiph. of נכה

25

(smite). Note the *tsere* to avoid three -*i*'s, DG 229 (note), WL 143, though this rule is not always followed.

לבדו, prep. *lamedh* plus noun בַּד (double-*ayin* root, and so with *dagesh* in *daleth* for suffixes) plus 3 m. s. suff. The form לְבַד is used almost always with suffixes to mean 'by himself', etc., lit. 'by his lonesome'.

Verse 3. וְאָשִׁיבָה, weak-*vav* plus 1 s. cohortative qal (with toneless *he*, *ayin-vav* verb) of שׁוּב (return), here transitive and therefore hiphil. 'And so I would bring back . . .'

אליך, prep. אֶל (to) plus 2 m. s. suff., looking like a plural, DG 70, WL 64ƒ.

כשׁוב . . . The rest of the verse is unintelligible. The EVV ignore the break which the Masoretes made at הכל (*zaqeph-qaton*), but even then do not achieve intelligibility. The Hebrew is 'when all return (the commentators usually translate "as the return of the whole"), the man whom thou art seeking, all the people shall be at peace', which might be intelligible if something were added to the middle clause, though even then the Hebrew would be somewhat abrupt. But LXX shows that the copyist probably omitted three words with a slight subsequent rearrangement to make sense (Dr 320). Read (or אַךְ) כְּשׁוּב הַכַּלָּה לְאִישָׁהּ רַק נֶפֶשׁ אִישׁ אֶחָד אַתָּה מְבַקֵּשׁ וְכָל־הָעָם . . . '(and I will bring back all the people to thee) as a bride returns to her husband: thou seekest but the life of one man'.

כשׁוב, prep. *kaph* ('as' or 'when') plus inf. cstr. qal of שׁוּב (return).

מבקשׁ, m. s. ptc. piel of בקשׁ (seek), piel and pual only found.

Verse 4. וַיִּישַׁר strong-*vav* plus 3 m. s. impf. qal of
יָשַׁר (to be smooth, straight, right), normal *pe-yod*
form. 'And (the word) was sound . . .'

וּבְעֵינֵי, *vav* (*shureq* before *beth*, DG 53, WL 44) plus
prep. *beth* plus cstr. pl. (dual) of עַיִן (eye).

זִקְנֵי, cstr. pl. of זָקֵן (beard, old man), 'elders of'.

Verse 5. קְרָא, 2 m. s. imperat. qal of קרא I (call,
read aloud), but the ancient Versions read the plural
קְרְאוּ, which is better.

וְנִשְׁמְעָה, weak-*vav* plus 1 pl. cohort. qal of שָׁמַע
(hear), equal to ἵνα.

בְּפִיו, prep. *beth* plus 1 s. suff. to sing. פֶּה (mouth),
DG 153, WL 186.

גַּם־הוּא. The personal pronoun reinforces the
suffix with emphasis, and this is doubled by the
insertion of גַּם (also), GK 135*f* and *h*, DS 1.

Verse 6. לֵאמֹר, prep. *lamedh* plus inf. cstr. qal of
אָמַר (say), in English idiom 'to wit', usually translated 'saying', probably because of the Greek λέγων,
λέγοντες, etc. The *chateph-seghol* under the guttural
has been swallowed up in the *tsere* under the *lamedh*,
DG 51, WL 44 (note).

דִּבֶּר, 3 m. s. pf. piel of דבר (say), a true perfect,
'has (just) said'. The *seghol* is found in the 3 m. s.
piel of three verbs only, דִּבֶּר (speak), כִּפֶּר (atone),
כִּבֶּם (wash clothes), GK 53*l*.

. . . אִם . . . הֲ, normal construction for alternative
question, GK 150*h*, DS 167*f*. For pointing of the
interrogative *he*: before gutturals-with-*qamets* the vowel
is *seghol*, before consonants with *sheva* and all other
gutturals it is *pathach*, otherwise it is *chateph-pathach*,
DG 167, WL 28*f*.

נַעֲשֶׂה, 1 pl. impf. qal of עָשָׂה (do), *pe*-guttural and *lamedh-he* verb.

אין, properly a noun meaning 'nothing', generally in cstr. אֵין, unless it is disconnected with what follows, as here. For disconnection, it is enough to be able to put a comma after it in English. As the accents in the text stand, the verse is to be translated as EVV, 'Shall we do his word? If not, thou speak', in which case אם is not part of an alternative question, but the hypothetical conjunction. If the *athnach* is moved from דברו to אין , then we have the break at אין , and can translate an alternative question, 'Shall we do his word or not? Thou speak.'

דבר, 2 m. s. imperat. piel of דבר (speak).

Verse 7. בפעם, prep. *beth* plus article plus פַּעַם (beat, footbeat, etc., and so 'occurrence' as here).

Verse 8. וּמָרֵי, *vav* (*shureq* before *mem*, DG 53, WL 44) plus cstr. pl. of מָר (bitter), the firm *qamets* because the root is double-*ayin*, and the *resh* cannot be doubled.

כדב, prep. *kaph* (like) plus דֹּב (bear), the masculine form being used of either sex. The root is double-*ayin*, so that the pl. is דֻּבִּים.

שַׁכּוּל, passive adjective 'bereaved', here cstr. sing.

בשדה, prep. *beth* plus article plus שָׂדֶה, which is the open country, uncultivated, but not wilderness. LXX adds καὶ ὡς ὗς τραχεῖα ἐν τῷ πεδίῳ, 'and like a savage (wild-) sow in the plain'.

ואביך, *vav* plus 2 m. s. suff. to sing. אָב (father), DG 153, WL 185.

ילין, 3 m. s. impf. qal of לִין (spend the night). The form לוּן is presupposed only by the inf. cstr. qal לוּן which occurs six times as against לִין once. All other forms are *ayin-yod*. Translate 'for he will not

28

spend the night with (prep. את) the people'. It is better to take the verb as a hiphil, 'for he will not let the people rest', את being now the sign of the direct definite object. This makes more sense, since the point is not that David himself will hide away from the rest, but that none of them will be asleep and they will be ready, from an ambush, to cause some initial slaughter among Absalom's men.

Verse 9. נחבא, m. s. ptc. niph. of חבא (hide), not the 3 m. s. pf. niph. 'Behold now (i.e. at this present moment) he is in hiding (lit. "is in a state of having hidden himself").'

באחת, prep. *beth* plus fem. cstr. of cardinal numeral 'one', though, since פחת is masc., we would expect the m. cstr. אחד, which indeed some read here.

באחד, prep. *beth* plus masc. cstr. of numeral 'one'. Some 40 MSS. read the fem. form, בְּאַחַת; indeed, מָקוֹם (place) is occasionally fem., probably under the influence of its plural in -*oth*.

והיה, strong-*vav* plus 3 m. s. pf. qal, 'and it will come to pass'.

כנפל, prep. *kaph* (when) plus inf. cstr. qal of נפל (fall). The normal construction is of the inf. cstr. with prep. and suffix, but here there is no suffix, the use being semi-impersonal, 'when there is a falling . . .' Note that the first syllable is open, and not closed, as with prep. *lamedh*, DG 77, WL 100, and especially GK p. 348 (note). There are two classes of *pe-nun* verbs: I, those like נגש, which assimilate the *nun* in the imperat. and inf. cstr. qal and have the vowel *pathach*, and II those like נפל, which keep the *nun* in the imperat. and inf. cstr. and also keep the *o*-vowel. The inf. cstr. qal and imperat. follow the impf. as usual. A general rule which will cover all

29

cases the beginner is likely to meet is that verbs like נפל II have a dental as the second radical, but נשׁך (bite) and נשׁק (kiss) vary.

בהם, prep. *beth* plus article (here *qamets*, DG 47, WL 36) plus demonstr. pronoun. It is better to read בָּעָם (among the people), following Lucian. Note that עַם with article becomes הָעָם, DG 45*f*, WL 27.

בתחלה, prep. *beth* plus article plus תְּחִלָּה (beginning).

והיה, strong-*vav* plus 3 m. s. pf. qal followed by act. qal ptc. with article: '(and it will come to pass . . .) that whosoever hears will say . . . (lit. "the hearer will hear and will say")'. The article refers to the particular man who is thought of as hearing and saying, WL 27 (§ 2*c*), GK 126*q*. For the idiomatic cognate subject, see GK 144*e*.

היתה, 3 f. s. pf. qal of היה, a true perfect: '(a slaughter) has taken place . . .'

Verse 10. והוא, 'and he', presumably the man-who-hears-and-says, but Lucian apparently read והיה (and it shall be), which is better, because the בֶּן־חַיִל (hero, brave man, lit. 'son of might') would not be likely to be disturbed by initial casualties.

־בֶּן, cstr. sing. of בֵּן (son), commonly used to denote one member of a group, type, whether animate or inanimate, GK 128*v*.

לבו, 3 m. s. suff. to sing. לֵב (heart). This noun has two forms, לֵבָב and לֵב, the latter being a double-*ayin* form and therefore having the form לִבּוֹ and other suffixes accordingly.

האריה, article (again the definite animal of which the writer is thinking, WL 27, GK 126*q*) plus אַרְיֵה (lion). This form is found in the sing. only, the

30

plural אֲרָיוֹת (17 times as against אֲרָיִים once)
being formed from אֲרִי, a distinct noun from אַרְיֵה.
This latter is found in Syriac, but the former in
Assyrian and Ethiopic.

The interpolation of a relative clause in this
manner is not common in Hebrew, the general pro-
cedure being to insert a short circumstantial clause,
e.g. 'and his heart is like the heart of a lion'. The
result of the intrusion of the relative clause is that
the verb ימס המס is removed unnaturally from its
subject, which is (presumably) 'the hero'.

המס, niphal inf. abs. strengthening the following
ימס, which is 3 m. s. impf. niph. (*pathach* lengthened
to *qamets* in pause) of the same root מסס (melt).
The niphal is used regularly, the only exceptions
being the qal in Isaiah x. 18 and the hiphil in
Deuteronomy i. 28. Translate 'will utterly melt away',
i.e. dissolve in fear. For the use of the inf. abs. to
strengthen the verb, DG 77*f*, and (more fully)
WL 101. Double-*ayin* verbs must always have one
consonant (radical) doubled, either the first or the
second. In the perfect it is always the second, and
in the imperf. both forms are found, the normal
Hebrew with the second doubled, and the Aramaizing
form with the first doubled. In the niph. impf. there
is no choice, since the first consonant is doubled in
any case. It is helpful, therefore, to think of the
3 sing. forms (for convenience) as הוּסַב הֵסֵב נָסֵב סַב,
יָסֹב and יִפֹּב, יָסֵב יִפַּב, יָסֵב and יַסֵּב, יוּסַב and יֵסֵב. Stative
double-*ayin* verbs have two forms in the impf. qal,
יֵקַל and יִמַּל.

Verse 11. כִּי must mean 'for', and can scarcely
here mean 'but', as EVV. Ehrlich suggested אָנֹכִי

31

('now I', to express emphasis), which is very good.

יעצתי, 1 s. pf. qal of יעץ (advise, counsel). A most vivid use of the perfect, 'of the immediate past' (DT 10), but it is even more immediate than that. According to ICC 351, it indicates that Hushai has thought it all out, and has come to a considered opinion, DG 155, § I, 1a (1).

האסף, inf. abs. niph. of אסף (gather), strengthening the following יֵאָסֵף, 3 m. s. impf. niph., 'let there be fully gathered'.

לרב, prep. lamedh (with qamets in the pretone, DG 53, WL 45) plus רב (multitude, abundance).

ופניך, vav (shureq before pe, DG 53, WL 44) plus 2 m. s. suff. of the plural פָּנִים (faces), here 'thy presence', a phrase used almost exclusively of God for reasons of reverence.

הלכים, m. pl. of הֹלֵךְ act. ptc. qal of הלך (go).

בקרב, prep. beth plus article (dagesh failing in qoph-with-sheva, DG 32f, WL 20) plus קְרָב (battle), an Aramaic word and late. It is better to read בְּקִרְבָּם ('in their midst', noun קֶרֶב) with the Versions.

Verse 12. ובאנו, strong-vav (shureq before beth, DG 53, WL 44) plus 1 p. pf. qal of בוא ('and then we will come').

נמצא, 3 m. s. pf. niph. of מצא (find), here equal to future perfect, 'where he shall have been found', DG 155, § I, 1a (4), GK 106o.

ונחנו, strong-vav plus 1 pl. pf. qal of נוח (settle, e.g. like the dew). This is better than taking it to be vav plus נַחְנוּ, a parallel form (cf. Arabic) of the pronoun אנחנו (we), translating 'and we (shall be) upon him'. Perles follows LXX παρεμβαλοῦμεν (and we shall camp), reading וְנָחֲנָה, weak-vav (which is bad here) plus 1 pl. impf. qal of חָנָה (encamp).

יִפֹּל, 3 m. s. impf. qal of נָפַל (fall), *pe-nun* verb class II, keeping *nun* in imperat. and inf. cstr. and retaining the -*o* vowel.

הָאדמה, properly אֲדָמָה, is the tilled earth, as against מִדְבָּר, the desert, and שָׂדֶה, the open, untilled land.

נוֹתַר, 1 p. impf. (jussive) hiph. of יתר (leave). The jussive is here used instead of the cohortative after the negative, GK 109*d*, DT 50. The normal 1 p. impf. hiph. is נוֹתִיר; the jussive would be נוֹתֵר, and with tone retracted נוֹתַר, as here, the *tsere* becoming *pathach* instead of *seghol* presumably because of the *resh*. But there is no reason why the form should not be regarded as 3 m. s. pf. hiph., 'and there shall not be left', thus avoiding all anomalies.

Verse 13. וְאִם, conditional sentence, 'but if וְאִם . . .', with the apodosis beginning at וְהִשִּׂיאוּ, pf. with strong-*vav*, 'then (all Israel) shall carry . . .', WL 205, DS 177, DT 136, GK 159*o*.

אֶל־עִיר, 'to a city', immediately following וְאִם for emphasis.

יֵאָסֵף, 3 m. s. impf. niph. of אָסַף (gather), here '(but if to a city) he shall withdraw himself'.

וְהִשִּׂיאוּ, strong-*vav* plus 3 p. pf. hiph. of נָשָׂא (lift up, carry, and in hiph. 'bring'). Many doubt this use of the hiphil, which is rare, and, following LXX, καὶ λήμψεται, read וְהֵבִיא (3 p. pf. hiph. of בּוֹא), 'and they shall bring'. Plural verb with sing. collective subject, WL 201, DS 159.

חֲבָלִים, pl. of חֶבֶל (cord).

וְסָחַבְנוּ, strong-*vav* plus 1 p. pf. qal of סָחַב (drag).

אֹתוֹ, 'him', ought to be fem. אֹתָהּ if it refers to

C 33

'city', which is fem., DG 56, WL 56. So Versions.

נמצא, 1 pl. impf. (future) qal, 'until we shall not find'.

צרור, this is from the root צרר III (to be sharp, whence a noun in Arabic, 'a sharp-edged stone'), and means 'pebble'. There is another word, צְרוֹר (bag), from צרר I (bind up).

Verse 14. טובה, f. s. adjective plus following מִן (comparative), '(is) better than . . .', DG 161, WL 31*f*.

ויהוה, the *chateph-pathach* of the *aleph* (perpetual Qere אֲדֹנָי) has been taken up in the firm *pathach* under the *vav*. The comment of the historian begins here, 'and so the Lord had commanded . . .'

צוה, 3 m. s. pf. piel of צִוָּה (only piel and pual found), here a pluperfect in that it was fore-ordained; 'had commanded, ordained'.

להפר, prep. *lamedh* plus inf. cstr. hiph. of פרר I (frustrate).

לבעבור, prep. *lamedh* (only thrice and pleonastically) plus בַּעֲבוּר, which acts as a prep., 'in order to', followed by inf. cstr.

הָבִיא, inf. cstr. hiph. of בוֹא (come), here 'bring' in English idiom, 'in order that the Lord might bring evil upon Absalom'.

Verse 15. כזאת וכזאת, 'thus and thus', BDB 262, being prep. *kaph* with *qamets* before the demonstrative (only thus with *kaph* and *beth*, WL 45, GK 102*g*).

אָנִי, pausal form with *silluq* at end of verse for אֲנִי, placed so for emphasis.

Verse 16. שלחו, 2 m. p. imperat. qal of שׁלח (send).

מְהֵרָה, properly noun meaning 'haste', but used as adverb. There are two very similar roots, מָהַר (to-

34

morrow) and מָהַר (haste), but the one with -h means 'hurry'.

וְהַפְּנִדוּ, weak-*vav* plus 2 m. p. imperat. hiph. of נגד ('tell').

תָּלֶן, 2 m. s. impf. (jussive) qal of לין (spend the night, tarry), תָּלֶן with tone retracted. אַל with jussive is ordinary command, but לֹא with impf. is strong prohibition, DG 83, WL 85 and 77.

בערבות, prep. *beth* plus cstr. pl. of עֲרָבָה (steppe) from ערב IV (to be arid). It is more likely that עַבְרוֹת (fords) was intended; cf. the Kethib of 2 Samuel xv. 28. The reference is probably to 'the fords of Jordan', Dr 316; cf. note above on עיפים, xvi. 14.

עבור, inf. abs. qal strengthening the following impf. qal, which acts as emphatic imperat., 'and what is more (וְנַם) be sure to cross over . . .'

יבלע, 3 m. s. impf. pual of בלע (swallow up), an impersonal passive construction, lit. 'lest it be swallowed up so far as the king is concerned', the *lamedh* being 'dative of reference'.

Verse 17. ויהונתן, the וִי is from an original וְיִ, DG 53, § 15, 1(*c*), Rem., WL 44, § 2(*c*).

עמדים, m. p. of act. ptc. qal of עמד (stand), 'were waiting'.

והלכה, strong-*vav* plus 3 f. s. pf. qal of הלך (go), consecutive from the participle, so that all the following verbs are frequentative: 'and the maid used to go, and tell them, and they (emphatic) would go and tell David'.

השׁפחה, article because it refers to the particular maid who went; cf. note on xvi. 6.

כי, 'because'.

יוכלו, 3 m. p. impf. qal of יָכֹל (to be able), DG 129, WL 138.

להראות, prep. *lamedh* plus inf. cstr. niph. of ראה, 'to be seen'.

לבוא, prep. *lamedh* plus inf. cstr. qal of בּוֹא (come), with *qamets* in the pretone, DG 53, WL 45, § 3(*b*), 1.

העירה, article plus עִיר (city) plus *he-locale*, the toneless *he* which is a relic of the old accusative ending, DG 61*f*, WL 211.

Verse 18. וירא, strong-*vav* plus 3 m. s. impf. (apoc.) qal of ראה (see), 'but a young man saw them . . .' The apoc. forms of this verb need special care, DG 147, WL 144. The tense sequence has changed to describe what happened on one particular occasion.

ויגד, strong-*vav* plus 3 m. s. impf. hiph. of נגד ('and he told'). The jussive form of the impf. hiph. is used, and not the impf. with -*i*, but the hiphil-*i* returns with suffixes.

וילכו, strong-*vav* plus 3 m. p. impf. qal of הלך (go), one of six *pe-yod* verbs like יֵשֵׁב.

שניהם, the cardinal number 'two', שְׁנַיִם (masc.) plus 3 m. p. suff., 'the two of them'.

ולו, *vav* plus prep. *lamedh* plus 3 m. s. suff., lit. 'and to him (i.e. the man in Bachurim)', a typical Hebrew circumstantial clause, but in English, 'now, he had a well . . .'

בחצרו, prep. *beth* plus 3 m. s. suff. plus חָצֵר (court).

וירדו, strong-*vav* plus 3 m. p. impf. qal of ירד (go down), one of the six special *pe-yod* verbs.

Verse 19. ותקח, strong-*vav* plus 3 f. s. impf. qal of לקח (take), DG 213, WL 255.

ותפרש, strong-*vav* plus 3 f. s. impf. qal of פרש (spread).

המסך, article (referring to the particular object,

36

GK 126*r*) plus מָסָךְ (covering); the root is double-*ayin*, but the first vowel is unchangeable, i.e. cstr. s. is מְסַךְ; cf. מָבְנֵי from מָגֵן (root נבן), DG 141 § 1(*b*), WL 190, GK 85*f*.

פְנֵי, cstr. pl. of פָּנִים (faces). Ten MSS. have פִּי (cstr. s. of פֶּה, 'mouth'), and it is a סְבִיר , i.e. a proposal known by the Masoretes, but not admitted as a Qere. C. D. Ginsburg argued that a Sebir was as sound as a Qere, but it actually is a reading which was definitely rejected by the Masoretes, even though often it makes better sense.

וַתִּשְׁחַט, strong-*vav* plus 3 f. s. impf. qal of שׁחט (spread out).

הָרְפוֹת. The word רִפָּה, of which רִפוֹת is the plural, is unknown. It is found only here and (with *yod* written full) in Proverbs xxvii. 22. LXX transcribed it, but the other Greek Versions make it παλάθας (cakes of compressed fruit), so Lucian and Theod., or πτισάνας (peeled barley), so Aq., Symm., and also Vulgate, but the Targum has 'dates'. It is evidently something that can be pounded in a mortar (Proverbs xxvii. 22) and dried in the sun. Qimchi has 'bruised corn', hence RV, which is as satisfactory as anything. See Dr 324.

נוֹדַע, 3 m. s. pf. niphal of ידע , 'and there was not known a thing'. The niph. ptc. has *qamets*.

Verse 20. הַבַּיְתָה, article plus בַּיִת (house) plus toneless *he-locale*. The *sheva* is open.

אַיֵּה, interrog. adverb, lengthened from אֵי (where?).

וַתֹּאמֶר, strong-*vav* plus 3 f. s. impf. qal with tone retracted.

מִיכַל, cstr. s. of מֵיכָל, perhaps 'brook', but meaning unknown. LXX has μικρὸν (a little). Ehrlich suggested

37

מִזֶּה אֶל־ (from here to); and Budde מְהֵרָה (hasten-ing), which has the support of Lucian and Vulgate. See Dr 325.

הַמַּיִם, article plus מַיִם (water), with *pathach* leng-thened to *qamets* in pause.

מָצְאוּ, 3 p. pf. qal of מצא (find), with tone re-tracted and in pause with *zaqeph-qaton*; normally מָצְאוּ.

וַיָּשֻׁבוּ, strong-*vav* plus 3 m. p. impf. qal of שׁוּב (return), 'so they returned'.

Verse 21. אַחֲרֵי, prep. 'after'; actually a cstr. dual form; cf. note on xvi. 8.

לְכְתָּם, inf. cstr. qal (לֶכֶת) of הלך (go) plus 3 m. p. suff., lit. 'after their going'; one of six verbs like יֵשֵׁב.

וַיַּעֲלוּ, strong-*vav* plus 3 m. p. impf. qal of עלה (go up, come up). *Pe*-guttural and *lamedh-he* verb.

מֵהַבְּאֵר, prep. מִן (from) plus article plus בְּאֵר. The word means a pit, or a well dug as against a natural spring, עַיִן.

וַיֵּלְכוּ, strong-*vav* plus 3 m. p. impf. qal of הלך (go), one of six verbs like יֵשֵׁב.

וַיֻּגַּד, strong-*vav* plus 3 m. p. impf. hiph. of נגד (tell, announce to). Note that the hiphil-*i* has re-turned; cf. note on verse 18.

קוּמוּ, 2 m. p. imperat. qal of קוּם (rise up).

וְעִבְרוּ, weak-*vav* (copulative) plus 2 m. p. imperat. qal of עבר (cross over).

Verse 22. וַיָּקָם, strong-*vav* plus 3 m. s. impf. qal of קוּם (rise up). The normal impf. form is יָקוּם; the jussive is יָקֹם, which, with tone retracted as here with strong-*vav*, becomes וַיָּקָם, *wăy-yấ-qŏm*, DG 131, § 2*b*, WL 158.

38

ויעברו, strong-*vav* plus 3 m. p. impf. qal of עבר (cross over). A normal *pe*-guttural form.

אור, usually parsed as cstr. sing. of the noun אור (light), 'until the light of morning', but the Targum evidently took it to be the cstr. inf. qal of the verb אור (be, become light), i.e. 'until the morning dawned'. This is less likely.

הבקר. The word בֹּקֶר properly means the point of time when the dark turns to light, just as עֶרֶב strictly means the point of time when the light becomes darkness. The root primarily means 'divide, split' (cf. Arabic), whence בֹּקֶר is that which splits the darkness, and בָּקָר (ox, cattle) is the animal which rips up, cleaves the soil, i.e. the ploughing animal.

The Masoretes divided the verse at 'Jordan', but Septuagint made the break at הבקר, which is more likely, and much easier.

אַחַד. This is one of six cases where the m. sing. cstr. appears instead of the normal absolute form, אֶחָד, GK 130*g*, and especially GK 96 (bottom of p. 282). Dr 325 thinks these forms are due to accidental corruption, but GK explains by the close connection with following phrase, thus being a construct in intention if not according to correct syntax. The position of the word makes it most emphatic, coming as it does before the negative. Kittel would read אֲשֶׁר, and follow the verb with אִישׁ, 'until there was not left a man', but it is best to retain the Masoretic text in spite of its unusualness.

נעדר, 3 m. s. pf. niph. of עדר III (to be lacking; cf. Arabic 'remain, lag behind', which is better here), but with the normal *pathach* changed to *qamets* in pause with *athnach*. DT 162 (note) would make the

39

form the niph. ptc. (cf. the *qamets*), and thus exceptionally construed with the negative לֹא (the normal negative with the ptc. is אֵין, GK 152*l*, DS 171*f*), but this is not necessary, though see GK 152*b*, DS 173.

עבר, 3 m. s. pf. qal, but here to be translated as a pluperfect.

Verse 23. The strong-*vav* sequence is broken when the interest turns back again to Achitophel, who knew that the rebellion must fail if David were once given the time to recover from the initial surprise.

נֶעֶשְׂתָה, 3 f. s. pf. niph. of עשׂה (do), *pe*-guttural and *lamedh-he* verb.

וַיְצַו, strong-*vav* plus 3 m. s. impf. apoc. piel of צוה (command), DG 147, WL 144; *dagesh* fails in *yod*-with-*sheva*, DG 32, WL 20. Here of his final commands before death; cf. 2 Kings xx. 1; in modern phrase, not the 'set his house in order' of RV, but 'made his will'. In modern Hebrew, צַוָּאָה means 'a will'.

וַיֵּחָנַק, strong-*vav* plus 3 m. s. impf. niph. of חנק (strangle), *pe*-guttural verb.

וַיָּמָת, strong-*vav* plus 3 m. s. impf. (jussive) qal of מות (die), with tone retracted. Pronounce *wǎy-yǎ́-möth*, DG 131, WL 158.

Verse 24. מַחֲנַיְמָה, toneless *he-locale* (relic of old accusative case ending, DG 61*f*, WL 211) plus מַחֲנַיִם, having *qamets* with *athnach* in pause. Presumably the vowel would be *pathach* out of pause, but this word with *he-locale* is always found in pause. A place-name, though the noun is a dual form meaning 'two camps'. The plural is מַחֲנוֹת.

40

Verse 25. שָׂם, 3 m. s. pf. qal of שׂוּם or שִׂים (set, appoint).

הַצָּבָא, article plus צָבָא (host). This is the militia, over which Joab was captain, i.e. of the army in the field, whereas Benaiah was captain of the king's body-guard of foreign mercenaries. The militia was the Israelite 'call-up'.

. . . וַעֲמָשָׂא, a circumstantial clause explaining Amasa's relationship to Joab. 'Now Amasa was the son of a man whose name (another little circumstantial clause) was . . .'

וּשְׁמוֹ, *vav* (*shureq* before *sheva*, DG 53, WL 44) plus 3 m. s. of sing. שֵׁם (name), a third declension noun, the first part being unalterable because it is not there, and the second part ending in *tsere* (or *cholem*). Both conditions must be fulfilled for a third declension noun.

הַיִּשְׂרְאֵלִי. This is strange. 1 Chronicles ii. 17 and LXX (Cod. A) have 'Ishmaelite'.

בַּת, cstr. sing. of בַּת (daughter), DG 153, WL 186.

אֲחוֹת, cstr. sing. of אָחוֹת (sister), DG 153, WL 185.

Verse 26. וַיִּחַן strong-*vav* plus 3 m. s. impf. (apoc.) qal of חָנָה (camp), *pe*-guttural and *lamedh-he* verb. Sing. verb with compound subject, WL 201, GK 146*f*.

Verse 27. כְּבוֹא, prep. *kaph* plus inf. cstr. qal of בּוֹא (come). The prepositions *beth* and *kaph* are used interchangeably to mean 'when he came', lit. 'in (at) his coming', DG 111, WL 100.

Verse 28. There is a verb missing which LXX supplies. Read הֵבִיאוּ ('brought') 3 m. p. pf. hiph. of בּוֹא (come), probably after יוּצַר, since the hiphil of בּוֹא is proper for animals and utensils, but the hiphil of נָגַשׁ (see הִגִּישׁוּ in next verse) is proper for food, i.e. 'brought near'. The EVV make the one verb apply to everything, as the Hebrew text, and insert it at the beginning of verse 28.

מִשְׁכָּב. Apparently they brought one bed only, for this word by itself must be translated 'a bed'. But LXX has δέκα κοίτας καὶ ἀμφιτάπους, i.e. 'ten couches and rugs'. Klostermann saw that the 'ten' was due to reading עֲשֶׂרֶת for an original עַרְשׂוֹת (cstr. pl. of עֶרֶשׂ, 'couch'), whence we may restore עַרְשׂוֹת מִשְׁכָּב וּמַרְבַדִּים 'and couches for lying down (lit. "couches of lying-down") and rugs'.

סִפּוֹת, pl. of סַף I (basin, goblet). It is a double-*ayin* root, whence the *dagesh* in the *pe*.

וּכְלִי, *vav* plus כְּלִי, which is sing. cstr. used as a collective noun. Perhaps read the cstr. pl., i.e. וּכְלֵי 'and potter's vessels'.

The plural חִטִּים means wheat in the grain, but the sing. חִטָּה is wheat in the ear. Similarly for 'barley', שְׂעֹרִים and שְׂעֹרָה, GK 124*m*, DS 19. The last word in the sentence is an accidental repetition, and is not found in LXX.

Verse 29. וְצֹאן (and sheep) is sound enough in itself, though some would insert חֶמְאַת to read 'sheep's milk', thus bringing this item into line with the rest, but cf. Lucian and Vulgate immediately below.

שְׁפוֹת. The word is unknown, and no satisfactory solution has been proposed. LXX transliterates the word, but Lucian and the Vulgate understood 'calves', but Syriac and the Targum have 'cheese', whence the EVV.

CHAPTER XVIII

Verse 1. וַיָּשֶׂם, strong-*vav* plus 3 m. s. impf. qal of שִׂים (set, appoint). The normal impf. is יָשִׂים ; the jussive is יָשֵׂם, which with tone retracted as here becomes *wăy-yắ-sĕm*, DG 131*f*, WL 158.

שָׂרֵי, cstr. pl. of שַׂר (prince, captain). The root is double-*ayin*, hence the firm *qamets* instead of a doubled *resh*.

Verse 2. וַיִּשְׁלַח, strong-*vav* plus 3 m. s. impf. piel of שׁלח (send), but Lucian read וַיְשַׁלֵּשׁ (and divided into three), a denominative verb from the numeral שָׁלֹשׁ (three), which is much more likely to be the original reading.

אֲחִי, cstr. sing. of אָח (brother), DG 153, WL 185.

יָצֹא, inf. abs. of יצא (go out, i.e. to battle) intensifying the following יֵצֵא, 1 s. impf. qal, DG 77*f*, WL 101. This verb is one of six like יֵשֵׁב.

Verse 3. The כִּי is 'because', and the אִם is 'if', with the apodosis beginning at לֹא־יָשִׂימוּ, 'they will not set heart to us', i.e. they will reckon nothing of us.

נֹס, inf. abs. qal of נוּס (flee), strengthening the following נָנוּס, 1 pl. impf. qal.

יָמֻתוּ, 3 m. p. impf. qal of מוּת (die).

חֶצְיֵנוּ, 1 pl. suff. plus sing. חֲצִי (half), a *lamedh-he* noun, DG 148, WL 189, GK 93*y*; 'and if half of us shall die', plur. verb with sing. collective noun.

עַתָּה, 'for now there are ten thousand as we', but it is better to read אַתָּה (thou) for עַתָּה (now) with LXX, Symm., Vulg., 'for thou art like us being ten thousand'.

מֵעִיר, prep. מִן plus עִיר (city), but read בָּעִיר (in the city) as LXX, or מֵהָעִיר (from the city).

לַעְזִיר. The Kethib is לַעְזִיר for לְהַעְזִיר (cf. GK 53*q*), prep. *lamedh* plus inf. cstr. hiph. of עזר (help), i.e. 'to bring help'. The Qere is לַעְזֹר, *lamedh* plus inf. cstr. qal 'to help', though Kittel suggests לְעֵזֶר (the noun, 'for help'), and ICC לְעֹזֵר (as a helper).

Verse 4. וַיִּיטַב, 3 m. s. impf. qal of יטב (to be good). There are three *pe-yod* verbs which always show the *yod*; they are 'If he *howls* יֵלֵל, let him *suck* יִנַק his thumb, and he will *be good* יֵיטַב'.

Verse 5. לָאַט, prep. *lamedh* plus אַט, which is a noun meaning 'gentleness', but is used only adverbially, generally with the preposition. Translate 'gently for me (לִי)', WL 207, § (*b*) ii, GK 119*s*.

לְאַבְשָׁלוֹם. This is in apposition to the previous לַנַּעַר. The prep. is sometimes repeated, especially when the first word is a proper name, GK 131*h*.

בְּצַוֺּת, prep. *beth* plus inf. cstr. piel of צוה (command), 'when the king commanded . . .'

Verse 6. לִקְרַאת, 'to meet'; see note on xvi. 1.

Verse 7. שָׁם (second) is probably an accidental repetition; similarly in verse 8.

After the number אֶלֶף (thousand), we would normally expect אִישׁ (men), as in LXX.

Verse 8. The Kethib נְפֹצֵות is probably an error, due to the accidental misplacement of the *vav*. Read the Qere נָפוֹצֶת, f. s. niph. ptc. of פוץ (to be scattered): 'and the fighting was being scattered . . .'

וַיֶּרֶב, strong-*vav* plus 3 m. s. impf. (apoc.) hiph. of רבה (to be many), followed idiomatically by

44

lamedh plus inf. cstr.; lit 'and the forest made many to devour among the people more than that which the sword devoured . . .', DS 113*f*.

Verse 9. וַיִּקְרָא, strong-*vav* plus 3 m. s. impf. niph. of קרא II=קרה (meet), lit. 'was met before . . .', i.e. accidentally met.

. . . וְאַבְשָׁלֹם, 'and Absalom (was) riding a mule', an idiomatic Hebrew circumstantial clause. Notice the mule is defined with the article, as being the particular mule he was riding.

שׂובֶךְ only here, meaning 'the interweaved (branches)', 'under the interwoven branches of the great oak (terebinth)', since the adjective is fem. and agrees with הָאֵלָה. Some would read הַגָּדוֹל, making the adjective refer to the branches, since שׂובֶךְ is masc. The oak is defined, because it is the particular oak in which he was actually entangled.

וַיֶּחֱזַק, strong-*vav* plus 3 m. s. impf. qal of חזק, a verb which has the sense of 'hold fast, hold tight, grasp firmly'.

וַיֻּתַּן, strong-*vav* plus 3 m. s. passive qal of נתן (set, give), DG 114 3(*c*), and not impf. hoph. as WL 131 probably intends, since there is no causative sense. But LXX, Syriac and Targum presuppose וַיִּתָּל (and he was suspended), strong-*vav* plus 3 m. s. impf. niph. of תלה , which is probably correct.

Verse 10. וַיַּרְא, strong-*vav* plus 3 m. s. impf. (apoc.) qal of ראה (see). The apocopated forms of this verb need particular care, DG 147, WL 144.

אִישׁ אֶחָד, 'a certain man'.

תָּלוּי, pass. ptc. qal of תלה (suspend, hang). The original final *yod* returns in this form regularly, DG 143, WL 143.

45

Verse 11. המגיד, article plus ptc. hiph. of נגד (tell), strictly 'to the man, the one that told him', and equal to the relative clause, WL 27, GK 126*b*.

והנה . . . . A good example of clauses which are co-ordinate in Hebrew, but where we would use 'if'; 'and behold (if) thou didst see, then (Heb. "and") wherefore did you not smite him . . .'

הכיתו, 3 m. s. suff. plus 2 m. s. pf. hiph. of נכה (smite).

ארצה, toneless *he-locale* plus ארץ (land, here 'ground'), but with the *pathach* lengthened to *qamets* in pause with *athnach*.

ועלי, 'and upon me', emphatic because of its position at the beginning of the clause.

לָתֶת, prep. *lamedh* plus inf. cstr. qal of נתן (give). The tone has been retracted, so that the *tsere* has become *seghol*, e.g. Genesis xv. 7; GK 20*h*.

Verse 12. ולא, follow the Qere ולוא for וְלוּ, 'even though I were weighing . . .'

שקל, act. ptc. qal of שקל (weigh). There is no need to read the pass. ptc., since the receiver weighs. DT 184 (class VI).

כפי, 1 s. suff. to dual of כף (palm of the hand): 'on my two hands'. There is no need to read the sing. כַּפִּי.

באזנינו, prep. *beth* plus 1 pl. suff. plus dual of אזן (ear); emphatic, 'for with our own ears . . .'

שמרו, 2 m. pl. imperat. qal of שמר (guard, take care of).

מי, if this can stand, it must mean 'whoever ye be', but it is better to follow the Versions with לִי (for me).

46

Verse 13. . . . אוֹ, 'or if (assuming another conditional clause beginning here, as though לוֹ were understood, GK 159*cc*) I had dealt deceitfully with his life (following the Qere)—and nothing can be hid from the king—then (DT 124, the apodosis begins here) thou (emphatic) wouldst have taken up thy stand aloof (i.e. from me)'. ICC would correct אוֹ to אִם, but actually לוֹ would be required here.

עָשִׂיתִי, 1 s. pf. qal of עשׂה (do), here to denote unfulfilled condition in the past, DS 179, DT 184 (class V).

בנפשו, the Qere is 'against my life', בְּנַפְשִׁי, i.e. 'or I would have done despite to my life', but in that case the last verb in the sentence would also need to be in the perfect.

יכחד, 3 m. s. impf. niph. of כחד (hide), but here translated by the auxiliary 'can', DS 64 § 43 (*b*), DT 41.

תתיצב, 2 m. s. impf. hithp. of צב (set, station oneself). BDB holds that the hithp. form is from the root יצב, as against other forms from the root נצב.

מנגד, the word נֶגֶד (properly a noun meaning originally 'conspicuous') has generally the sense of hostility, oppositeness. It means 'flat in the face of', as against לִפְנֵי, which means 'in front of' without any sense of opposition or contradiction, e.g. Psalm xxiii, 5; 'thou preparest a table before me (לפני, in front of me), flat in the face of (נגד, in spite of) my adversaries'.

לא כן אחילה, 'not sowill I tarry (before thee)', i.e. I have no time to waste with you. LXX has two renderings, the second is as the Hebrew οὐχ οὕτως μενῶ, but the first is διὰ τοῦτο ἐγὼ ἄρξομαι, and is found also in Lucian and Targum, i.e. לָכֵן אָנֹכִי אָחֵלָּה,

47

'therefore I (emphatic) will begin before you (place)'.
Both readings are good.

אחילה, 1 s. impf. (cohort) hiph. of יחל (wait).
The suggested אָחֵלָּה (see previous note) is 1 s. impf.
(cohort) hiph. of חלל (begin, profane). This verb
has two hiphils, the Hebrew double-*ayin* form, which
doubles the second (and third) radical, pf. הֵחֵל and
impf. יָחֵל, meaning 'begin', and the Aramaizing
double-*ayin* form יָחֵל, which doubles (by impli-
cation) the first radical, found only in impf. and
meaning 'profane' (transitive).

שבטים, 'rods', but it is better to follow LXX, βέλη
(darts), i.e. שְׁלָחִים; so most moderns.

ויתקעם, strong-*vav* plus 3 m. s. impf. qal of תקע
(smite) plus 3 m. p. suff.

עוֹד, properly a noun meaning 'continuance', but
used as an adverb 'yet'. Here with 3 m. s. suff.,
DG 136 (note), WL 110*f.*

חי, m. s. adj. (alive) from root חיה.

Verse 15. ויסבו, strong-*vav* plus 3 m. p. impf. qal
(Hebrew form with second radical doubled) of סבב
(go round, surround); normal double-*ayin* form.

נשאי, cstr. pl. of נֹשֵׂא, act. ptc. qal of נשׂא (carry).

ויכו, strong-*vav* plus 3 m. p. hiph. of נכה (smite).

וימיתהו, strong-*vav* plus 3 m. p. impf. hiph. (יָמִיתוּ)
of מות (die) plus 3 m. s. suff.

Verse 16. ויתקע, strong-*vav* plus 3 m. s. impf. qal
of תקע (smite, or of a trumpet as in verse 14, 'blow').

שׁפר, the curved trumpet of ram's horn.

וישב, strong-*vav* plus 3 m. s. impf. qal (יָשׁוּב,
jussive יָשֹׁב) of שׁוב (return) with tone retracted,
and pronounced *wăy-yā́-shŏv*, DG 131, WL 158.

48

מרדף, prep. מִן (from) plus inf. cstr. qal of רדף (pursue). The *dagesh forte* has failed in *resh-with-sheva*; cf. also 1 Samuel xxiii. 28. GK 102*b*, 22*s* demands the *dagesh* in both cases, but it is not so according to the best texts.

Verse 17. וַיִּקְחוּ, strong-*vav* plus 3 m. p. impf. qal of לקח (take), with *dagesh* failing, as usual, in *qoph-with-sheva*, DG 32*f*, WL 20.

וַיַּצִּבוּ, strong-*vav* plus 3 m. p. impf. hiph. of נצב (set up). See note on verse 13.

נָסוּ, 3 p. pf. qal of נום (flee). Notice accent: נָסוּ is *ayin-vav* form, but גָּלוּ is *lamedh-he*.

Verse 18. 'Now Absalom had taken (pf. translated as pluperfect).'

וַיַּצֶּב־, strong-*vav* plus 3 m. s. impf. hiph. (יַצִּיב, jussive יַצֵּב) of נצב (set up), with vowel shortened into *seghol* before *maqqeph*. The effect of the *maqqeph* (DG 40, WL 28, 118) is to make the whole phrase one, so that in this case the vowel must be short, since now it is in a closed syllable before the tone.

בְחַיּוֹ, prep. *beth* plus חַיִּים (plur. noun 'life') plus 3 m. s. suff.

מַצֶּבֶת. This properly is the cstr. sing. of מַצֵּבָה (pillar, stele), but see later in verse. It is unusual to find את without the article, wherefore most would read הַמַּצֵּבָה (the stele). LXX found the Hebrew difficult and is confused.

בַּעֲבוּר, used as a prep. before the inf. cstr. hiph., 'in order to cause (men) to remember my name'.

עַל, here 'according to', BDB 754*a*. LXX omits this and the following words to לה; not necessary so to do, though it makes the text easier.

וַיִּקָּרֵא, strong-*vav* plus 3 m. s. impf. niph. of קרא

(call), used impersonally, lit. 'and there was called to it . ר .'

יד, 'hand', but used here, as in 1 Samuel xv. 12, to mean 'sign, monument'.

Verse 19. ארוצה, 1 s. impf. (cohort. with toneless *he*) qal of רוּץ (run).

ואבשׂרה, weak-*vav* plus 1 s. impf. (cohort.) piel of בשׂר (announce). The root means 'make smooth', whence 'make smooth the face with good news', and בָּשָׂר, 'flesh', from the smoothness of the skin.

שׁפטו, 3 m. s. pf. qal of שׁפט (judge, but here 'judged favourably', 'given him the verdict', and almost 'saved') plus 3 m. s. suff.

Verse 20. ובשׂרת, strong-*vav* plus 2 m. s. pf. piel, 'but thou shalt tell good news . . .'

אחר, 'another', the *cheth* is virtually doubled; hence the first vowel remains short.

כן is read, but not written; the Masoretes evidently realized that it had been accidentally omitted. כי על כן is a pleonastic phrase for כִּי, 'because'.

מת might be either the act. ptc. qal or the 3 m. s. pf. qal (probably the latter) of מוּת (die).

Verse 21. לֵךְ, 2 m. s. imperat. qal of הלך (go), one of six verbs like יֵשֵׁב.

הגֵּד, 2 m. s. imperat. hiph. of נגד (tell).

ראיתה, 2 m. s. pf. qal of ראה (see), with final vowel written full.

וישׁתחו, strong-*vav* plus 3 m. s. impf. (apoc.) hithpalel of שׁחו(ה) (bow down). The original final *vav* has been retained, and the final *he* added; usually the *he* is substituted for the *vav* to make a true *lamedh-he* verb. This verb needs care, especially in respect of the apocopated forms, DG 145, WL 145. The transposition of the *tau* and the *shin* is normal, DG 93, WL 72.

כּוּשִׁי, here a proper name, but previously not so. Read הַכּוּשִׁי, 'the Cushite'.

וַיָּרָץ, strong-*vav* plus 3 m. s. impf. qal of רוּץ (run). The tone is not retracted here because of the pause, the jussive form being retained.

Verse 22. וַיֹּסֶף, strong-*vav* plus 3 m. s. impf. hiph. of יסף (add). Care is needed to distinguish between the forms of יסף (add) and אסף (gather).

וִיהִי, weak-*vav* plus 3 m. s. juss. qal of היה (be). The normal jussive is יְהִי. The *dagesh* has failed in *yod*-with-*sheva*; then the *sheva* has failed under the *yod*, so that we are left with a long-*i* written full, DG 147*f*, WL 145: 'let come what (may)'.

זה, emphatic enclitic, 'why on earth are you to run', DS5, Rem. 2, GK 136*d*.

רָץ, act. ptc. qal of רוּץ (run), 'about to run', *fut. instans*, DS 134, GK 116*d*.

בני, noun בֵּן plus 1 s. suff., DG 153, WL 186.

וּלְכָה, *vav* (*shureq* before vocal *sheva*, DG 53, WL 44) plus לְךָ written with final vowel full, 'and to thee'.

מֹצֵאת, fem. sing. act. ptc. qal of מצא (find). Some moderns point מֻצֵאת, fem. sing. of hoph. ptc. of יצא (go out), i.e. 'no reward for good tidings will be brought forth to thee'. Perhaps it is a corruption of the וַיֹּאמֶר which the Versions rightly find at the beginning of the next verse.

Verse 23. רוּץ, 2 m. s. imperat. qal of רוּץ (run).

וַיָּרָץ, strong-*vav* plus 3 m. s. impf. qal of רוּץ (run); normal impf. is יָרוּץ, jussive is יָרָץ, and with tone retracted, as here, וַיָּרָץ, pronounced *wăy-yā́-rŏts*: 'so he ran . . .', DG 131, WL 145.

51

Verse 24. הַצֹּפֶה, article plus צֹפֶה, act. ptc. qal of צפה (look out), here used as a noun, 'watcher'.

רָץ, act. pts. qal of רוּץ (run).

אֶל־הַחוֹמָה, 'to the wall', perhaps עַל, 'upon. . .'

וַיִּשָּׂא, strong-*vav* plus 3 m. s. impf. qal of נשׂא (lift up).

Verse 25. בְּפִיו, prep. *beth* plus פֶּה (mouth) plus 3 m. s. suff., DG 153, WL 186.

וַיֵּלֶךְ הָלוֹךְ וְקָרֵב, lit. 'and he went, going and being near', an idiomatic Hebrew construction for 'he kept on getting nearer and nearer'. The normal construction is finite verb (הלך, or some such verb) followed by its own inf. abs. and then another inf. abs., but here the last word is the act. ptc. instead of קָרוֹב the inf. abs.; an alternative is to use two participles instead of the two inf. absolutes; cf. 2 Samuel iii. 1; DS 119*f*, WL 101, GK 113*s*.

Verse 26. אֶל־הַשֹּׁעֵר, 'to the porter (gate-man)', but it is better to follow Lucian and Syriac with אֶל־הַשַּׁעַר, 'to the gate'.

אִישׁ (second), add אַחֵר (another) with LXX and Syriac.

Verse 27. מרוצת, cstr. sing. of מְרוּצָה (running).

. . . וְאֶל־בְּשׂוֹרָה, 'to a good reward he will come', but Targum suggests 'and what is more, good news he will bring', וְאַף בְּשׂוֹרָה טוֹבָה יָבִיא, which is better.

Verse 28. וַיִּקְרָא, 'and he called', but Lucian read וַיִּקְרַב (and he drew near), which is better.

לְאַפָּיו, prep. *lamedh* plus the dual אַפַּיִם (lit. pair of nostrils) plus 3 m. s. suff.; 'face to the ground'. The *lamedh* is unusual in this common phrase, and is probably an error from the previous word.

52

סִגַּר, 3 m. s. pf. piel of סגר (shut), with *pathach* in last syllable because of the *resh* (equal to guttural).

Verse 29. שָׁלוֹם. The Masorah was against the reading הֲשָׁלוֹם, but noted that it was a suggested alternative (Sebir). It would certainly make better sense: 'is it well with the youth . . . ?'

לִשְׁלֹחַ, prep. *lamedh* plus inf. cstr. qal, though prep. *kaph* or *beth* would be more usual. Translate 'when Joab sent the king's servant and thy servant', but most moderns would read, 'when Joab sent thy servant', לִשְׁלֹחַ (כִּשְׁלֹחַ) יוֹאָב אֶת־עַבְדְּךָ, regarding the rest as glosses.

Verse 30. סֹב, 2 m. s. imperat. qal of סבב (go round).

הִתְיַצֵּב, 2 m. s. imperat. hithp. of יצב, 'station thyself, take up thy stand'; see note on verse 13.

Verse 31. בָא, m. s. act. ptc. qal of בוא after הִנֵּה (behold).

יִתְבַּשֵּׂר, 3 m. s. impf. (jussive) hithp. of בשׂר, 'let my lord the king receive good tidings'.

שְׁפָטְךָ, 3 m. s. pf. qal plus 2 m. s. suff.

הַקָּמִים, article plus m. plur. of קָם, act. ptc. qal of קוּם (arise).

Verse 32. יִהְיוּ, 3 m. p. impf. (jussive) qal of היה (be).

CHAPTER XIX

Verse 1. וַיִּרְגַּז, strong-*vav* plus 3 m. s. impf. qal of רגז (to be agitated violently), used of earthquakes and great disquiet.

וַיַּעַל, strong-*vav* plus 3 m. s. impf. (apoc.) qal of עלה (go up).

וַיֵּבְךְ, strong-*vav* plus 3 m. s. impf. (apoc.) qal of
בכה (weep). For this unusual apocopated form, see
DG 147, WL 144.

בְּלֶכְתּוֹ, prep. *beth* plus inf. cstr. qal לֶכֶת of הלך
(go), 'as he went', but Lucian read בִּבְכֹתוֹ, *beth* plus
inf. cstr. qal of בכה (weep), which is perhaps better.

מִי־יִתֵּן, lit. 'who will give . . .', i.e. 'O that . . .',
WL 203, GK 151*d*, DS 183.

מוּתִי, inf. cstr. qal of מות (die) plus 1 s. suff., not
the noun, which would be מוֹתִי.

אֲנִי, the personal pronoun emphasizing the suffix,
DS 1, GK 135*e-h*.

תַּחְתֶּיךָ, dual form plus 2 m. s. suff. (instead of,
properly 'underneath').

Verse 2. וַיֻּגַּד, strong-*vav* plus 3 m. s. impf. hoph.
(here a true passive of the hiphil) of נגד, 'and it
was told . . .'

וַיִּתְאַבֵּל, strong-*vav* plus 3 m. s. impf. hithp. of אבל
(mourn). Some suggest the ptc. מִתְאַבֵּל, but a strong-
vav with impf. is found occasionally following a ptc.
which describes a present state, DT 92; unless per-
chance it means 'and hath gone into mourning'.

Verse 3. וַתְּהִי, strong-*vav* plus 3 f. s. impf. (apoc.)
qal of היה in its true sense, 'and the victory hath
become . . .'

נֶעֱצַב, 3 m. s. pf. niph. of עצב (to pain), 'the king
hath been sore pained on account of his son'. Ptc.
niph. has final *qamets*.

Verse 4. וַיִּתְגַּנֵּב, strong-*vav* plus 3 m. s. impf. hithp.
of גנב (steal), i.e. 'got themselves away like thieves',
this preserving the hithpael sense of reflexive re-
iteration.

לָבוֹא, prep. *laemdh* (*qamets* before tone syllable,

54

DG 51, WL 45) plus inf. cstr. qal (WL 45) of בוא
(come).

הנכלמים, art. plus m. pl. of ptc. niph. נִכְלָם of
כלם (to be humiliated), defining the sing. collective
noun 'people', acting as a relative clause.

בנוסם, prep. *beth* plus inf. cstr. qal of נוס (flee) plus
3 m. p. suff.

Verse 5. לאט, 3 m. s. pf. qal of לוט (wrap tightly).
The *aleph* is unusual though original to the root (cf.
Arabic), and the word should probably be pointed
לָאט. The second המלך should probably be omitted
with the Versions.

Verse 6. הבית, article plus בַּיִת (house), with *qamets*
for *pathach* in pause. Some MSS. read the usual
he-locale הַבָּיְתָה, but this is not essential.

הבשת, 2 m. s. pf. hiphil of בוש (to be ashamed),
intransitive in the qal, but transitive in the hiphil,
as here. The true *ayin-vav* hiphil would be הֵבִישׁ and
so הֵבִישׁׁתָ, but this is formed as if the verb were יבש
(*pe-vav*), i.e. הוֹבִישׁ and הֹבַשְׁתָּ, DG 152, GK 78*b*.

הממלטים, article with *dagesh* failing in *mem*-with-
sheva (DG 32, WL 20) plus m. p. of piel ptc. of מלט.
Word really means 'slip through', and it is used of
'escape' intransitively in the niphal, but 'let escape,
deliver' transitively in the piel. See *Exp. Times*,
July, 1944, p. 266.

נשיך, 2 m. s. suff. to נָשִׁים, plural of אִשָּׁה (woman,
wife), DG 153, WL 185.

פלנשיך, 2 m. s. suff. to plural of פִּלֶגֶשׁ (concubine); see note on xvi. 21.

Verse 7. לאהבה, prep. *lamedh* plus inf. cstr. qal of

55

אָהֵב (love); cf. DG 81, WL 99; lit. 'to love . . .', or, in English idiom, 'by loving'.

שֹׂנְאֶיךָ, 2 m. s. suff. to plural·of שֹׂנֵא, act. qal ptc. of שָׂנֵא (hate).

There are three different uses of the conj. כִּי in this verse: first and third 'for'; second and fourth 'that'; fifth resumptive, GK 157, 158.

אֵין לְךָ, usually means 'thou hast no princes . . .', but the meaning intended is 'princes and servants are nothing אֵין to thee'.

לֹא, the Qere לוּ is correct, hypothetic clause, unfulfilled condition in the past and (here) up to the present: 'if Absalom had been alive . . .'

Verse 8. . . . קוּם, three 2 m. s. imperatives.

דַבֵּר עַל לֵב, lit. 'speak to the heart of . . .'; cf. Isaiah xl. 1; Genesis xxxiv. 3 (woo).

נִשְׁבַּעְתִּי, 1 s. pf. niph. of שָׁבַע (swear), always niph. in this sense; e.g. St. Patrick's hymn, 'I bind myself'.

כִּי אֵינְךָ, the sebir inserts אִם (if), but it is deliberately omitted, lest there be confusion with the following אִם, which introduces the substance of the oath. 'For (the first כִּי) I swear by the Lord that (the second כִּי) if thou are not now (force of the ptc.) going out, assuredly (אִם introducing the oath) not a man will lodge. . . .' As in English oaths, positive oaths have a negative form, and vice versa; e.g. 'I am . . . if I do' means that I will not, whilst 'I am . . . if I don't' means that I will.

וְרָעָה, strong-*vav* plus 3 f. s. pf. qal of רָעַע (to be evil).

בָּאָה, with accent on the first syllable is 3 f. s. pf. qal; the f. s. act. ptc. qal has the accent on the last syllable.

מִנְעָרֶיךָ, prep. מִן plus 2 m. s. suff. to נְעָרִים, a plural form which denotes a time of life, GK 124*d*; here 'youth'.

Verse 9. וַיֵּשֶׁב, strong-*vav* plus 3 m. s. impf. qal of יָשַׁב (sit), with tone retracted and short vowel in last syllable.

וְיִשְׂרָאֵל, the *vav*-consecutive is broken, 'but Israel fled . . .'

Verse 10. . . . וַיְהִי כָל, 'and all the people were in a state of striving together', GK 51*d*. נָדוֹן is niph. ptc. of דִּין (strive).

הִצִּילָנוּ, 1 p. pf. hiph. of נָצַל (deliver) plus 1 pl. suff.

וְהוּא, 'and he' emphatic.

מִלְּטָנוּ, 1 p. pf. piel of מָלַט (let escape) plus 1 pl. suff.

פְּלִשְׁתִּים, always without the article.

Verse 11. מַחֲרִישִׁים, m. p. of hiph. ptc. of חָרַשׁ (to be silent).

לְהָשִׁיב, prep. *lamedh* plus hiph. inf. cstr. of שׁוּב (return).

Verse 12. . . . וּדְבַר, 'and the word of all Israel came . . .', Syriac, with many LXX and some Vulgate MSS., transposes this phrase to the end of the previous verse, where it certainly makes good sense.

Verse 13. אָחִי, 1 s. suff. to אָחִים plural of אָח (brother), DG 153, WL 185.

Verse 14. וְלַעֲמָשָׂא, 'and to Amasa (in particular) . . .', placed first for emphasis.

תֹּמְרוּ, 2 m. p. impf. qal for תֹּאמְרוּ, GK 68*h*.

. . . כֹּה יַעֲשֶׂה, a type of oath found in Samuel and Kings; see Dr on 1 Samuel iii. 17; here 'so may God

57

do to me, and so may he add'. In Jezebel's mouth, the word אלהים is construed as a plural, meaning heathen gods. יעשׂה is strangely the ordinary imperf. and not the jussive. יסיף is 3 m. s. impf. (again not jussive) hiph. of יסף (add).

אם לא, introducing the substance of the oath, which is positive in intention, the negative being used, DG 168*f*, WL 201*f*.

Verse 15. וַיֵּט, strong-*vav* plus 3 m. s. impf. (apoc.) hiphil (and so transitive) of נטה (incline). Lucian inserts 'Amasa' as subject; Targum assumes וַיֵּט, i.e. the qal, and makes 'heart' the subject, in which case the את־ must be deleted.

Verse 16. עד־הירדן, 'up to the Jordan'. This river is always '*the* Jordan'.

הגלגלה, also always with the article, except in this case twice only, Joshua v. 9, xii. 23. Here with toneless *he-locale*.

ללכת, prep. *lamedh* plus inf. cstr. qal of הלך (go). Ten MSS. read לרדת (to go down), inf. cstr. of ירד, the more usual description of a journey down into the Jordan Valley, e.g. to Jericho.

לקראת, from קרא II (meet); see note on xvi. 1.

Verse 18. The first four words belong to the previous verse. The rest of this verse and the first half of verse 19 is the story of Ziba, after which the story of Shimei is resumed.

חמשת עשר, the חֲמֵשֶׁת f. s. cstr. form is unusual (here and Judges viii. 10 for 15; Judges xx. 25 for 18), the normal form being the f. abs. followed by the masc. עשׂר when used with masc. nouns, DG 164. WL 195, and especially GK 97*e*.

וצלחו, weak-*vav* plus simple perfect, but this is irregular, and in any case the syntax here demands

58

the omission of the *vav*, which has come from dittography (see previous word). צלח means 'leap, rush' and is used to describe the timely zeal of Shimei, and the speed with which he sought to atone for his previous 'previous' conduct.

Verse 19. ועברה העברה is usually translated 'and the ferry-boat kept passing over', but this meaning for עֲבָרָה is not confirmed elsewhere, and the word usually means 'crossing, ford'. LXX has a doublet here, reading the present Hebrew text for the second, but ועברו העברה for the first, whence Wellhausen suggested וְעָבְרוּ הָעֲבָרָה, 'and they kept crossing the ford', which is good. Both ועברה and ועברו are strong-*vav* with perfects, intended as frequentatives. See Dr. 335.

בעברו, prep. *beth* plus inf. cstr. qal of עבר (cross) plus 3 m. s. suff. The vowel is a short-*o* and the *sheva* is vocal, DG 102, WL 100. See RV margin.

Verse 20. יחשׁב־, 3 m. s. impf. (jussive) qal of חשׁב (consider, reckon). The last vowel is short-*o* before *maqqeph*, being now in a closed syllable before the tone, DG 40, WL 28.

העוה, 3 m. s. pf. hiph. of עוה II (denominative from עָוֹן, meaning 'commit iniquity').

. . . לשׂום, 'for the king to take it to heart'.

Verse 22. ויען, strong-*vav* plus 3 m. s. impf. (apoc.) qal of ענה (answer).

התחת, interrog. *he* plus prep. תַּחַת (here 'instead of').

יומת, 3 m. s. impf. hoph. of מוּת (die).

Verse 23. מה־לי ולכם. Cf. note on xvi. 10.

לשׂטן, prep. *lamedh* plus שָׂטָן, here 'adversary'. For further development of this word, see the commentaries on Job, HDB iv. 407–412, etc.

. . . היום יומת, either a question, presumably indicated by the lifting of the voice, or an oath, positive in form and therefore with a negative to be introduced, here without the imprecatory אִם.

Verse 24. וַיִּשָּׁבַע, strong-*vav* plus 3 m. s. impf. niph. (as usual) of שבע (swear), with tone retracted.

Verse 25. רַגְלָיו 3 m. s. suff. to רַגְלַיִם, dual of רֶגֶל (foot).

לֶכֶת הַמֶּלֶךְ must be in apposition to הַיּוֹם, since הַיּוֹם has article and therefore cannot be in construct to the clause.

Verse 26. יְרוּשָׁלַם. Read either 'from Jerusalem' or transfer to the end of the previous verse.

הָלַכְתָּ, 'didst thou (not) go', i.e. in the original flight.

Verse 27. רִמָּנִי, 3 m. s. pf. piel of רמה (beguile) plus 1 s. suff., but notice the *qamets* in pause instead of the normal *pathach*.

אֶחְבְּשָׁה-לִּי, 1 s. cohort. qal of חבש (bind, and so 'saddle'); 'let me saddle me', but the Versions make it a command to his servant, חֲבָשָׁה-לִּי לוֹ '(thy servant said) to him, Saddle me . . .' חֲבָשָׁה is 2 m. s. (emphatic) imperat. qal; the first vowel is short-*o*, and the *sheva* is vocal.

וְאֶרְכַּב, weak-*vav* plus 1 s. impf. qal of רכב (ride). We would expect the cohortative here, and also in the following verb.

עָלֶיהָ, prep. עַל plus 3 f. s. suff., but it ought to be 3 m. s. suff., since חֲמוֹר is the he-ass.

אֶת-. Many MSS. read אֶל-, which is easier.

Verse 28. וַעֲשֵׂה, weak-*vav* plus 2 m. s. imperat. qal of עשה (do).

Verse 29. כִּי אִם introduces an exception after a negative, GK 163*a, c*.

וַיָּשֶׁת, strong-*vav* plus 2 m. s. impf. qal of שִׁית (set, place). The normal impf. is יָשִׁית, jussive יָשֵׁת, and with tone retracted as here, יָשֶׁת.

שׁלחך, the tone is retracted in pause with *athnach*, so that the vocal *sheva* under the *nun* has become *seghol*.

צדקה, here 'right, claim'.

ולזעק, 'and to cry . . .', but this is difficult. Either omit the *vav* or follow Lucian with וַיִּזְעַק, 'and he cried (further) . . .', which is good in view of the next verse.

Verse 30. תדבר. Lucian presupposes תַּרְבֶּה, 'why do you multiply words?'

Verse 31. יקח, 3 m. s. impf. qal of לקח (take), but with *qamets* for *pathach* with *athnach* in pause.

Verse 32. The natural meaning of the Hebrew is 'and he (Barzillai) crossed Jordan with the king to escort him לשׁלחו', but did Barzillai really cross the river? Probably not, so that here עבר means 'pass on to'. If Barzillai did cross the river, then they may be right who would read וַיַּעֲבֵר המלך את־הירדן, 'and the king caused (him) to cross the Jordan'.

את־בירדן cannot be right. It is probably a conflation of את־הירדן and בירדן. Lucian has 'from the Jordan'. The last two words are difficult, and possibly should be omitted as a gloss.

Verse 33. והוא, 'and he it was who', emphatic.

כלכל, 3 m. s. pf. pilpel of כּוּל (contain), with meaning 'nourish', but the final vowel in this case is *pathach*, and not *tsere*, as the grammars suggest, WL 160, GK 55*f*, 72*m*.

בשיבתו, prep. *beth* plus שִׁיבָה (sojourn) plus 3 m. s. suff. The noun is explained as a shortened form of וְשִׁיבָה, from the root ישׁב, but it is better to follow LXX and read בְּשַׁבְתּוֹ ('when he sojourned', *beth* plus inf. cstr. qal of ישׁב plus suffix), though, as ICC says, the author may have intended בְּשִׁבְיתוֹ (in his exile).

Verse 34. וְכִלְכַּלְתִּי, strong-*vav* plus 1 s. pf. pilpel of כּוּל ('and I will nourish thee').

Verse 35. שְׁנֵי, cstr. pl. of שָׁנָה (year). The plural שָׁנוֹת is rare, mostly poetic and late; cf. especially Deuteronomy xxxii. 7, which had great influence, since the two Songs of Moses (Deuteronomy xxxii and Exodus xv) have been Sabbath Canticles from a very early date.

Verse 36. הַאֵדַע, interrog. *he* plus 1 s. impf. qal of ידע (know), 'do I know (i.e. can I distinguish)?' followed by אִם to make the alternative question, according to rule, DG 168, GK 150*g*.

יִטְעַם, 3 m. s. impf. qal of טעם ('can thy servant taste'), DS 64, GK 107*r*.

אֹכַל, 1 s. impf. qal of אכל (eat), shortened from אֹאכַל, and the regular form for the five *pe-aleph* verbs.

שָׁרִים, m. p. of שָׁר, act. ptc. qal of שִׁיר, which is a denominative verb from שִׁיר (song), and followed by the f. p., 'singing men and singing women'.

לְמַשָּׂא, prop. *lamedh* plus מַשָּׂא (burden). The *dagesh* in the *sin* is because the root is נשׂא, *pe-nun* verb. It is better followed by עַל, as LXX, ἐπί.

אֶשְׁמַע בְּקוֹל, Dr 337 rightly distinguishes between שָׁמַע בְּ (listen to) and שָׁמַע without prep., which is 'hearing' without appreciation.

Verse 37. כִּמְעַט, lit. 'like a little', and with impf. 'just'. Thus 'Thy servant will just cross Jordan with the king', but this use is not found elsewhere, and so many follow Lucian, כִּי מְעַט, 'for thy servant will just . . .', which is sound. But did Barzillai ever cross the river? If not, then translate עבר 'pass on' and omit 'the Jordan' as a gloss by a scribe who thought the verb meant 'cross over', or make the verb a hiphil

וַיַּעֲבֹר, and translate, 'For thy servant will just escort the king across the Jordan', in which case אֶת־הַיַּרְדֵּן should follow אֶת־הַמֶּלֶךְ. See Dr. 337.

There is no need for the 'it' of the English Versions.

Verse 38. יָשֹׁב־, 3 m. s. jussive qal (יָשֹׁב) of שׁוּב (return), with short-*o* because of following *maqqeph*: 'let, I pray thee, thy servant return, and I will die'.

There is a break in the sentence at כִּמְהָם (with accent *rebhia*): 'but behold thy servant Kimham, let him cross over'.

Verse 39. תִּבְחַר עָלַי, '(which) thou shalt choose (to lay as an obligation) upon me'.

לָךְ, prep. *lamedh* plus 2 m. s. suff. but in pause, DG 51 (note), WL 49.

Verse 40. עָבַר, 3 m. s. pf. qal with final *qamets* in pause, but Lucian and some LXX MSS. read עָמַד (stayed, stood, tarried), which is good.

וַיִּשַּׁק, strong-*vav* plus 3 m. s. impf. qal of נשׁק (kiss), which sometimes, as here, acts like נגשׁ and has imperfect in -*a*. Similarly נָשַׁךְ (bite); cf. note on xvii. 9.

וַיְבָרְכֵהוּ, strong-*vav* plus 3 m. s. impf. piel of ברך (bless) plus 3 m. s. suff. There is great dispute as to whether the *resh* in such forms of ברך should have simple *sheva* or *chateph-pathah*. Sephardi (Spanish) MSS. have the *sheva*, and Ashkenazi (Eastern) MSS. have the *chateph-pathach*. The best MSS. and editions vary from case to case.

וַיָּשָׁב, strong-*vav* plus 3 m. s. impf. qal (tone retracted, and short-*o* in last syllable) of שׁוּב (return).

Verse 41. כִּמְהָן. Elsewhere the name is Kimham.

וַיְעֱבִרוּ, the Kethib is וַיַּעֲבִרוּ, 'and they brought (the king) across', which could stand if the previous phrase were joined to the first half of the verse, but

63

the Qere is better, וַיַּעֲבִרוּ. וי is often mistaken for ה by translators. But LXX translates עֹבְרִים, which is best of all.

Verse 42. נָבוֹךְ, 3 p. pf. qal plus 2 m. s. suffix.

Verse 43. זה, the enclitic use for emphasis; cf. xviii. 22.

חָרָה לְךָ, impersonal 3 m. s. pf. qal, lit. 'it is hot to you', i.e. 'are you angry'.

הַאָכוֹל, interrog. *he* plus inf. abs. qal strengthening the following 1 p. pf. qal. The אם of the disjunctive question follows.

נִשֵּׂאת is difficult. It is best to read either the sing. מַשְׂאֵת (portion; cf. Genesis xliii. 34) or the plural מַשְׂאֹת, with the meaning, 'have we received any special favour?', lit. 'has there been brought a portion to us?' This is the interpretation of Targum. The difficulty arises partly from the expectation of another inf. abs., but the niph. inf. abs. should be נִשֹּׂא, GK 76*b*. Klostermann suggested נִשֵּׂא נָשֹׂא, 'or are we at all carrying (him) away for ourselves?' See Dr 339 for further details.

Verse 44. יָדוֹת. This is the true plural of יד (hand); the dual is יָדַיִם. The meaning here is 'parts'.

וְגַם־בְּדָוִד, 'and also I am in David more than you', but LXX has πρωτότοκος, i.e. בְּכוֹר, 'firstborn', the rest of the doublet representing the Hebrew text.

הֲקִלֹּתַנִי, 2 m. s. pf. hiph. of קלל ('make light') plus 1 s. suff. Note the *pathach* under the *tau*, which is regular. Some MSS. and printed edd. have *chateph-seghol* under the *he*, but the best texts have *chateph-pathach*.

וַיִּקֶשׁ, strong-*vav* plus 3 m. s. impf. qal of קשׁה (to be hard, fierce). The corresponding hiphil form is יַּקְשֶׁ.

לי is unnecessary, and may be due to a dittograph.